The House Is Made of Poetry

Ad Feminam: Women and Literature
Edited by Sandra M. Gilbert

 WITHDRAWN

The House Is Made of Poetry
The Art of Ruth Stone

*Edited by Wendy Barker
and Sandra M. Gilbert*

Southern Illinois University Press
Carbondale and Edwardsville

PS
3 537
.TL 817
Z68
1996

"Poetry and Life, Poetry and Ruth," copyright © 1996 Jan Freeman.

Illustration on title page, photo of Ruth Stone by Jan Freeman © 1995.

All quotations from the poetry of Ruth Stone are reprinted by permission of
Ruth Stone.

"Mapping Ruth Stone's Life and Art" by Wendy Barker is taken from the
Dictionary of Literary Biography, Volume 105. Edited by R. S. Gwynn, Lamar
University. Copyright © 1991 Gale Research, Inc.

"An Interview with Ruth Stone: 1990" by Robert Bradley originally appeared in
the AWP Chronicle 23.2 (Oct.-Nov. 1990). Reprinted courtesy AWP Chronicle.

A version of "The Poetry of Ruth Stone" by Norman Friedman was originally
published in Contemporary Poets, St. James Press, 1991. Reprinted courtesy St.
James Press.

"An Interview with Ruth Stone: 1973" by Sandra M. Gilbert originally appeared
in California Quarterly 10 (Autumn 1975): 55–70. Reprinted courtesy California
Quarterly.

Library of Congress Cataloging-in-Publication Data
The house is made of poetry : the art of Ruth Stone / edited by Wendy
    Barker and Sandra M. Gilbert.
        p.   cm. — (Ad feminam)
    Includes bibliographical references (p.   ) and index.
    1. Stone, Ruth—Criticism and interpretation. 2. Women and
literature—United States—History—20th century.   I. Barker,
Wendy.   II. Gilbert, Sandra M.   III. Series.
PS3537.T6817Z68   1996
811'.54—dc20   95-17839
ISBN 0-8093-2012-6   CIP

7596

Contents

Ad Feminam: Women and Literature

> Ad Hominem: to the man; appealing to personal interests, prejudices, or emotions rather than to reason; *an argument ad hominem.*
> —*American Heritage Dictionary*

Until quite recently, much literary criticism, like most humanistic studies, has been in some sense constituted out of arguments *ad hominem*. Not only have examinations of literary history tended to address themselves "to the man"—that is, to the identity of what was presumed to be the *man* of letters who created our culture's monuments of unaging intellect—but many aesthetic analyses and evaluations have consciously or unconsciously appealed to the "personal interests, prejudices, or emotions" of male critics and readers. As the title of this series is meant to indicate, the intellectual project called "feminist criticism" has sought to counter the limitations of *ad hominem* thinking about literature by asking a series of questions addressed *ad feminam:* to the woman as both writer and reader of texts.

First, and most crucially, feminist critics ask, What is the relationship between gender and genre, between sexuality and textuality? But in meditating on these issues they raise a number of more specific questions. Does a woman of letters have a literature—a language, a history, a tradition—of her own? Have conventional methods of canon-formation tended to exclude or marginalize female achievements? More generally, do men and women have different modes of literary representation, different definitions of literary production? Do such differences mean that distinctive male- (or female-) authored images of women (or men), as well as distinctly male and female genres, are part of our intellectual heritage? Perhaps most important, are literary differences between men and women essential or accidental, biologically determined or culturally constructed?

Feminist critics have addressed themselves to these problems with increasing sophistication during the last two decades, as they sought to revise, or at times replace, *ad hominem* arguments with *ad feminam* speculations. Whether explicating individual texts, studying the oeuvre of a single author, examining the permutations of a major theme, or charting the contours of a tradition, these theorists and scholars have consistently sought to define literary manifestations of difference and to understand the dynamics that have shaped the accomplishments of literary women.

As a consequence of such work, feminist critics, often employing new modes of analysis, have begun to uncover a neglected female tradition along with a heretofore hidden history of the literary dialogue between men and women. This series is dedicated to publishing books that will use innovative as well as traditional interpretive methods in order to help readers of both sexes achieve a clearer consciousness of that neglected but powerful tradition and a better understanding of that hidden history. Reason tells us, after all, that if, transcending prejudice and special pleading, we speak to, and focus on, the woman as well as the man—if we think *ad feminam* as well as *ad hominem*—we will have a better chance of understanding what constitutes the human.

Sandra M. Gilbert

Preface
Outside the Poetry Factory

Her words are alive, write the commentators whose essays on Ruth Stone appear here. Her house is made of poetry. Her intense attention to the ordinary transforms it into (or reveals it as) the extraordinary. Her passionate verses evoke impassioned responses.

Ruth Stone's vitality, intensity, and dedication to art are recurrent themes throughout this collection of tributes to her life and work. Her sense of the comic is bittersweet, framed in darkness, some remark; her tragic insights, others show, are outlined in light. And all agree that as a sort of pilgrim of poetry, she has stubbornly persisted in making and remaking language under even the most difficult, often painfully daunting circumstances, recording the stages of grief with icy clarity while always celebrating what is alive, what endures.

Critic and cultural historian Leslie Fiedler, one of Stone's earliest admirers, observes that readers have lately "appeared in ever grow-ing numbers" to appreciate her work; yet, as Fiedler goes on to note, it is "almost miraculous that it has happened at all in light of the fact that Ruth Stone has never been a member of any school or clique or gaggle of mutual admirers." Similarly, Sharon Olds comments that Stone's "unusual lack of self-promotion has resulted in her work being slow to find its readers," which makes it all the more remarkable that "in their originality and radiance" her poems have finally begun to "shine in their place within her generation, among the pioneering women (Bishop, Brooks, Rukeyser)."

That Stone's "lack of self-promotion" results from a conscious refusal rather than an inadvertent oversight, that in her case (as in

Marianne Moore's rather different one) "omissions are not accidents," becomes quite clear in the sardonic vision of "the poetry factory" at the heart of her hilarious "Some Things You'll Need to Know Before You Join the Union." "At the poetry factory," the piece begins, "body poems are writhing and bleeding" when "Mr. Po-Biz himself comes in from the front office" (*S-HC* 49). Later,

> They're stuffing at the poetry factory today.
> They're jamming in images
> saturated with *as* and *like*.
>
> (*S-HC* 50)

In the end, though, the monitory fate of an aspiring po-biz star reveals what Stone sees as not just the futility but the madness of aesthetic self-marketing:

> In the poetry factory
> it's very hot.
> The bellows are going,
> the pressure is building up.
> Young poems are being rolled out
> ready to be cut.
> Whistles are blowing.
> Jive is rocking.
> Barrels of thin words line the walls.
> Fat words like links of sausages
> hang on belts.
> Floor walkers and straw bosses
> take a coffee break.
> Only the nervous apprentice
> is anywhere near the machines
> when a large poem
> seems about to come off the assembly line.
> "This is it," the apprentice shouts.
> "Get my promotion ready!
> APR, the quarterlies,
> a chapbook, NEA,
> a creative writing chair,
> the poetry circuit, Yaddo!"
> Inside the ambulance
> as it drives away
> he is still shouting,
> "I'll grow a beard,

become an alcoholic,
consider suicide."

(S-HC 50–51)

Like most recent American poets, Ruth Stone has done her share of teaching. Indeed, this collection offers celebrations of her pedagogical as well as her poetic art by a number of former students and disciples. Yet taken together, the essays included here consistently testify to Stone's radical unworldliness, in particular her insouciant contempt for the "floor walkers and straw bosses" who sometimes seem to control the poetry "factory" both inside and outside the university. Rather than surrender herself to the schools and cliques of po-biz operators and their hangers-on, Stone has devoted herself to the severe and humble listening she describes in the beautiful conclusion of *"Liebeslied"*:

> I remember my father
> whistling late at night.
> He is walking along Irvington Avenue
> from the streetcar line.
> Alone, downstairs
> he winds up the phonograph—
> at the wavering edge
> Fritz Kreisler's *Liebeslied*.
> I listen in the dark
> to the bowed strings of sadness and pain
> to what the human voice
> beyond itself
> is telling me.

(S-HC 13–14)

Perhaps the exuberant austerity of Stone's vocation is best dramatized by the titles of three of her major collections: *Cheap* (1972), *Second-Hand Coat* (1987), and *Simplicity* (1995). In the ordinary sense, there is nothing cheap or second-hand about this poet's art, yet her poems focus on the simplicity of pains and pleasures that are cheap as air, second-hand as the heritage every writer receives from literary tradition. At the same time, as the critics represented here assert in many different ways, the eloquence, complexity, and subtlety of Stone's rich oeuvre reveal the wealth of inspiration she has found waiting for her in the darkness of the *Liebeslied*, outside the poetry factory.

In order to trace the relationship between Ruth Stone's own *Liebeslied* and what she elsewhere calls "the blood and meat of the world" (*WM* 59), we have organized this book into three sections. The first, "Knowing Ruth Stone," offers memoirs by writers of different generations who have known the poet well over the years, with Leslie Fiedler testifying to her singularity ("She resists all labels"; is "one of the few contemporaries whom it is possible to think of simply as a 'poet'"), Sharon Olds defining her vitality ("A Ruth Stone poem feels alive in the hands"), and Jan Freeman praising her aesthetic intensity ("Everything in the life of Ruth Stone is integrated with poetry").

Our second section, "A Life of Art," is meant to familiarize readers with the outlines of Stone's career and to offer an overview of her poetic evolution. Wendy Barker and Norman Friedman both discuss the writer's movement from the high spirits and elegant craft of her first volume, *In an Iridescent Time* (1959), through the deepening shadows that mark the strongly shaped poems of her later collections—*Topography* (1970), *Cheap*, and *Second-Hand Coat*—to the poignant wit of *Who Is The Widow's Muse?* (1991) and the bittersweet meditations of *Simplicity*, her most recent book. Next, in two interviews—one from the nineties and one from the seventies—Robert Bradley and I record the poet's own sense of her aesthetic origins and her literary growth.

Then, in our third section, "Reading Ruth Stone," we gather essays examining a range of Stone's key themes and modes. Diane Wakoski and Diana O'Hehir focus in particular on the comic—or more precisely *tragi*comic—vision that colors much of her work, while Kevin Clark and Elyse Blankley survey the explicitly political aspects of her art and Roger Gilbert analyzes her often uncannily astute insights into the "otherness" of other lives. And finally, drawing on the biographical background of the "grief-work" Stone has done in most of her books, both Janet Lowery and Kandace Brill Lombart examine the verse she has produced "under the seal of my widowhood," and I study the *caritas*, the empathic love, that redeems pain in so many of her poems.

As we assembled these essays, Wendy Barker and I were aided, advised, and encouraged by a number of friends and associates. In particular, we would like to thank John Beckman, Susan Gubar, Lisa Harper, Bob Phillips, Chris Sindt, Valerie Thornberry, each of the contributors to this volume, and—especially—Ruth Stone herself. We join all the writers represented here in our gratitude for Ruth Stone's faith in poetry and our appreciation for the intensity of her commitment to act on that faith. "I sit with my cup / to catch the crazy falling alphabet" (*S HC* 4), she has written, as if to describe the position she long ago staked out for herself outside the walls of the poetry factory, and it gives us joy to think that there, in a space where even the "bowed strings of sadness and pain" become jubilant with art, she hears and transcribes

> what the human voice
> beyond itself
> is telling me.

Sandra M. Gilbert

Abbreviations of Collections of Poetry by Ruth Stone

C   *Cheap*. New York: Harcourt, 1972.

IT   *In an Iridescent Time*. New York: Harcourt, 1959.

S-HC   *Second-Hand Coat: Poems New and Selected*. Boston: Godine, 1987; Cambridge, MA: Yellow Moon, 1991.

Sim   *Simplicity*. Northampton, MA: Paris, 1995.

Sol   *The Solution*. Towson, MD: Haw River, 1989.

TOP   *Topography and Other Poems*. New York: Harcourt, 1970.

WM   *Who Is the Widow's Muse?* Cambridge, MA: Yellow Moon, 1991.

Part I   *Knowing Ruth Stone*

As a poet she was a great hunter . . . keen, joyful, beautiful, rakish and eerie by moonlight.

—Sharon Olds

I   *On Ruth Stone*
Leslie Fiedler

I have been reading and passionately responding to Ruth Stone's poetry for more than half a century, ever since I rescued and deciphered a balled-up, scribbled page that she had tossed under the bed in her tiny pre-fab house just off Harvard Yard. Though she occasionally read one aloud to her family and closest friends, she had still—in that irrecoverable time of our shared youth—made no attempt at publishing her poems. It was as if, at that point, it was enough for her simply to have written down the words that echoed in her head—to have made real and external what had hitherto remained imaginary and internal.

To be read by strangers (much less honored and loved by them) was, it seemed to me then, something she did not yet dare to dream; or at least did not yet dare to confess she dreamed. But over the years such readers have, of course, appeared in ever growing numbers. That is to say, the private voice I was for a while among the few privileged to overhear has become—for better or worse—a public voice. Not only is it heard from platforms all up and down the land; but fixed in print, it is also peddled in bookstores and preserved in libraries.

All this has happened slowly, to be sure, but I find it almost miraculous that it has happened at all in light of the fact that Ruth Stone has never been a member of any school or clique or gaggle of mutual admirers. Nor has she subscribed to any of the fashionable modes that category-loving critics are so eager to tout. In fact, she resists all labels, being not a "confessional poet," a "language poet," a "formalist poet" old or new—not even, despite the womanliness of every line she writes, a "feminist poet."

She is, that is to say, one of the few contemporaries whom it is possible to think of simply as a "poet": one of a distinguished company going back to Chaucer or Sappho, who slough off all qualifying modifiers, belonging not to an age but the ages. What earns her this distinction is in the first place the language of her verse, which despite its wit and precision is never far from the colloquial. But it also is the product of her subject matter, which is rooted in the commonplace: the small joys and griefs of being a mother and a daughter, a lover, a wife and widow.

In any case, the parameters of the world she evokes are domestic rather than cosmic. When she leaves the kitchen and the bedroom, it is only to walk in the woods, work in the garden, hang up the wash, or sing under a familiar sheltering sky. Amazingly, though, she is never banal. She makes us aware, rather, as if for the first time, of what we have always known but somehow forgotten: the wonder of the ordinary, the ordinariness of wonder.

2 *Ruth Stone and Her Poems*
Sharon Olds

A Ruth Stone poem feels alive in the hands—ardent, independent, restless. A Stone poem propels forward like a gifted wide-end receiver—it has "broken field" (the ability to change course, instantly, at speed, left or right, with great precision); it swivels its hips and *moves*.

Ruth Stone's poems are mysterious, hilarious, powerful. They are understandable, often with a very clear surface, but not simple—their intelligence is crackling and complex. Her poems are musical, and their music is unforced, unlabored-over, fresh.

In my midteens I had the joy of meeting Ruth Stone through my cousin, the poet and editor A. T. McIntyre, and in my late teens and early twenties I had the blessing of visiting Ruth and her daughters in Vermont. She gave me a vision of a genius at work. She herself seemed to be the location of a *daimon*; she was a place where life turned into art. She was a woman who chopped wood for hearth fires, and hauled water, in winter, from the river—first hacking a hole in the ice with an ax. She was a great beauty (with a great West Virginia melodious mountain cackle) who wore old softened blue jeans and men's (one beloved man's) Oxford shirts. The beam of her attention was extremely bright, warm, and encouraging, and she was *in love with* poetry.

I saw her living a life of poetry that was communal—not that she sought readers out in the greater world; she did not seem to send poems to magazines, or books to publishers—but readers were there, in the living room, in Brandon, Vermont. When you were there you felt yourself to be in the heart of the poetry family.

The great sweeping beams of her eyes, the great sweeping beams of her heart, softly raked the earth, the house. Her senses seemed acute as an owl's. In one way she seemed the persona of a shapely warm-blooded small mammal, a snowy marten, perhaps, or a snow-shoe hare—not a predator but one of the predated upon—but as a poet she was a great hunter, noiseless, keen, joyful, beautiful, rakish and eerie by moonlight, and her poems were alive, vivid: *they* were the owls. (Now I remember that there was an owl in that house—a stuffed owl, in the study of her late husband, the poet Walter Stone. When I saw it I thought of a revenant, and of Minerva, goddess of knowledge sought and unsought.)

One blizzardy Christmas I spent in Vermont with Ruth and her family. What larks! I love the pair of pink waffled cotton bloomers that were one of the treats in my stocking (which had a felt hearth, and felt fire, and felt candelabra on it). Every day for hours we'd play the Poetry Game—everyone would think up one word, then we'd pool them, then we'd write poems each of which contained all the pooled words. The food and the dishes would run out at about the same time, and we'd keep going on tea and imagery.

Ruth, a great, generous appreciator, could see the spark of life in each poem. I remember her ferocious doting *attention* when one read, her childlike pleasure and focus, her joy in poetry, her need of it, and the beauty of her body, girlish and voluptuous, as she sat and listened—and her catty humor, and her wonder.

She is a poet of tragedy, and she is a jaunty poet, not proper, her work without middle-class prudishness. She is a poet of great humor—mockery even—and a bold eye, not obedient. There is a disrespect in her poems, a taken freedom, that feels to me like a strength of the disenfranchised.

Ruth's poems are direct and lissome, her plainness is elegant and shapely, her music is basic, classical; it feels as real as the movement of matter. When we hear a Stone first line, it is as if we have been hearing this voice in our head all day, and just now the words become audible. She is a seer, easily speaking clear truths somehow unmentioned until now. And one has the sense of enough air in her poems—they lift up.

I love Ruth Stone's irony, and the melody of her irony. In many of her poems we hear the music of the quiet, deep unhopefulness of the poor, the unfooled.

The things in Stone's poems are often ordinary and transcendent at the same time. Ruth has a kind of bald religious sense that is also political. She has sometimes the sound of a prophet. She gives us visions of the uses of power. She looks at the police, and the academics; she looks at gender and race and class, and she judges. They are the judgments of one who had had higher hopes for the human.

Ruth Stone also "dance[s] the diddy on a wrinkled knee" (*IT* 45)—she has a lovely quality that approaches the silly, the "dirty." She has, sometimes, something of a snicker, a mocking note about sex. Her sharp focus is not blurred by ladylikeness. She has a canny lack of respect; she makes fun of what is pompous. Sometimes her making fun is slightly merciless, or bitter—a tit-for-tat sharpness toward a male academic, or a male surgeon. She has a savage cosmic vision. Her savagery is often feminist savagery—she is always for the earth, for the harmed mother.

Stone is bold and rich in describing the plants and things of the earth, and she does not overdescribe them so that they become literary artifacts rather than natural things. When she transplants them to the page, they keep their size and shape, and their roots don't die—she recognizes their principle of integrity, so their livingness survives over.

Stone has the image imagination. She seems to think in images, to easily visualize the invisible. She has a tragic deadpan humor: love and destruction are right next to each other.

Ruth Stone's voice is unsentimental. She has tremendous accuracy, tremendous pleasure in the thing-as-it-is, even when it is unpleasant, ridiculous, pathetic. And the *things* that dance in her books! The filing cases of wizened eggs! The furnace ducts!

In Ruth Stone's work there is wisdom, and there is reckless ballading. There is a lack of fear of the grotesque—mortality makes for the grotesque.

The premises of many of the poems are unusual. Often, their domestic location is fresh. And she has a vision of the bazook— she gives us the grim humor of ordinary awful misery. Ruth Stone strikes me as hilariously and seriously anti-middle-class, seeing through class pretensions and refusals. Sometimes her poems go into a daring realm almost of nonsense-talk—sometimes she Does Nonsense. It embodies the foolishness of hope, the stupidity of vanity and orderliness. One approaches, in it, the outskirts of a huge bitterness, which sings.

From the earliest poems, we see her effortless gift for musical language. Over time, the music has become more and more complex, as if she dances with her brain as much as with her feet. So much necessity came along, in her imagination and her subjects, and her art was so equal to it, that the poems were compressed into a severe tragic-comic genius; they often remind me of matter transformed by forces in the natural world. Stone seems to have a deeply grounded sense of space and time. She gives enough time to the colloquial sentence; she lets it stretch out and have its natural time along the lines. She has a fine sense of how long things take, of duration—how time feels, passing.

Ruth Stone's poems, in their originality and radiance, their intelligence and music and intense personal politics, shine in their place within her generation, among the pioneering women (Bishop, Brooks, Rukeyser). Her unusual lack of self-promotion has resulted in her work being slow to find its readers. But her readers are passionate in their respect and love and amazement over her poems—the poems' energy, freshness, and spunk, their speaking to our lives. This volume should help more of us find her; we are hungry for her. Ruth Stone's poems are the food the spirit craves, the lasting nourishment Lousie Bogan referred to when she said, "Here's a crumb of hereafter." Stone gives us loaves and loaves of hereafter, of Adamant here and now.

3 *Poetry and Life, Poetry and Ruth*
Jan Freeman

The house is made of poetry. The walls are covered with books. Surfaces, stacked with notebooks. Piano, tables, typewriter, shelves, floors. Record jackets and old grocery lists, covered with drafts of poems. On the bathroom walls, poems by students, friends, her children, grandchildren. For years an early poem by Sharon Olds hung beside the light switch. Now, Mother's Day poems beside drawings and photos of Ruth, her children, grandchildren, friends and students. Everywhere, something connected to poetry.

"Listen to this," she says on the phone, and reads "Scheherazade Is Mailed and Nailed in Five Days." It is a poem that blows the roof off. "I just finished this last version. I took most of the Holocaust references out. Let me read it to you and tell me what you think, if it works." It is a poem that is entirely emblematic of this period in history. A poem about the death of the storyteller, the death of culture, the dying world, changing reality. And it is an autobiographical poem about her own life, her relationship to her husband and her husband's spirit. At nine o'clock in the morning, on the telephone, I listen to a major American poem. A landmark. And later, "Do you have a minute? I just read this poem in an anthology and it creates the smells of spring. Listen . . . " and she reads Billy Collins's poem "Tuesday, June 4, 1991" from Louise Glück's *Best American Poetry of 1993* anthology. "I wish more poetry would do that—evoke your senses, the euphoria that life gives you when you are strong, happy, and healthy."

9

Everything in the life of Ruth Stone is integrated with poetry. Poetry and life. Poetry and Ruth.

We are sitting in front of the cast-iron cookstove in her kitchen in August. A chilly night in Vermont. Her granddaughter, Bianca, asleep in a chair, having read us six new poems after our supper. Poems, she says, influenced by Grandma's poems "Coffee and Sweet Rolls" ("I love that poem, don't you?") and "Plumbing." Now Ruth goes through her new manuscript, *Simplicity*, reading the titles aloud, and reading poems. Shifting the order. The kitchen is warm, the fire in the stove radiates heat, poems like the steam from the pots, filling the room. And then talk about other poets (this one is sick, this one is better now and happy, this one thought their poems were similar and she wishes they'd known each other better) and more poems. The next morning we make apple jelly. We sterilize the jars and the lids in big pots on the cookstove. We trim crabapples and apples, listening to Italian folktales on the tape recorder. Apples from the tree in "Green Apples." "Remember that poem?" she asks. "The apples you and Bianca picked are from the tree in that poem."

Laundry, toys, visitors, neighbors, the food in the cupboard, aisles in the supermarket, conversations with children, grandchildren, views from a bus, from her Binghamton apartment—everything turns into poems or threads toward poems as the great Mother Poet in the Goshen house stirs the jelly in the cast-iron pot. Either you love poetry and you love Ruth or you pack up and head back down the mountain. Past the black dog and the sheep in the woods, the pond by the road and the sign to Brandon. The intensity in this Goshen house offers little room for a middle ground. It's passion in the web or out you go in a passion.

In the aura of the house, the aura of Ruth Stone, there is often the presence and absence of Walter Stone—his name in conversation, his image in icons, in stories by Abigail Stone and lithographs by Phoebe Stone, two of Ruth's daughters. And of course there is Ruth's poignant and astonishing *Who Is the Widow's Muse?*, a book that pays tribute to the life of the widow, the act of survival, through grief and humor, and finally resolution. *Widow's Muse* reveals the tragic and hilarious detail of mourning, living through loss, the ongoing relationship between the widow, her dead husband, and death's mark of desertion.

"This is where the children slept in summer," she says, pointing to the back porch off the kitchen. Twenty years later, the daughters with their own children stop by from their nearby homes in Middlebury and Whiting. Marcia arrives with Nora, the spitting image of Ruth as a young woman. "Can you believe I ever looked like that? But I did! I've got the pictures to prove it!" Choke cherries, red currants, the clothesline tied between the apple trees out back. Charles Pork, Ruth's short-legged, long-bodied dog, asleep beside the front door.

I stayed in the house the summer after I studied with Ruth at NYU. When I arrived with another NYU student and her eight-year-old son, we were offered the upstairs rooms. For two months, we played the Poetry Game, wrote poems, read poems, cooked pots of spaghetti, pushed the two-year-old twins in an old wicker carriage up and down the dirt road in front of Ruth's house. Bells and chimes on the front porch. Petunias. The picnic table. The linen cupboard filled with sheets and winding sheets.

"After Walter's death I bought dozens of sheets. All different kinds. Some were beautiful linens with lace. Some were embroidered. Years later I realized they were winding cloths. To wrap his body."

"At night I am reading *The Egyptian Book of the Dead*."

"Once I was driving to Connecticut and the wall opened. I was suddenly among, suddenly a part of the universe. Everything was reaching, breathing, ascending. That was the most amazing amazing experience of my entire life. It came to me uninvited. I've heard that people who meditate wait for years for something like that to happen and often they never experience it. A wall in my mind wasn't there suddenly. I knew the life of everything. Never again did I not feel that I was not among. It extended to everything. I never felt the same about anything. The universe is a living being."

"We are no different from a blade of grass or a beetle."

"Everything fights for itself, but everything loves to be loved," she says, sitting in the wicker chair, rubbing Bianca's foot.

"I'm trying not to be mortal. That's why I'm writing all these plastic poems," she says on the phone after announcing she'll be seventy-nine this June [1994].

She is upstairs writing in the room with Bianca's desk and the dolls and mouse house. Or she is lying in the bed in the room beside the living room, reading physics, reading astronomy. The house of poetry is a world of cells, black holes, microorganisms, children, grandchildren, dogs, cats, students. Outside, the birds singing loudly. They fill the bushes and they fill the trees. Upstairs, the squirrels and mice scurry through the attic, behind the walls. The house is alive. Poetry is everywhere.

It is early in the morning, Ruth stands in a nightgown, hair down, a cup of coffee in one hand—"Listen to this poem I wrote last night" or "I found this in a notebook just now—tell me what you think" or "Read me something from your notebook—let me hear what you were working on yesterday."

At night, in summer, sleeping on the screened-in porch, mattresses dragged out—for a breezier evening—waking with birdsong, hanging plants hanging from the roof, clay pots, wicker thrones, the sound of chimes.

Echoes of her drummer father. Her mother on the mountain, hip broken. Unfamiliar with the country life then, Ruth hiked down to her oil tank at the bottom of the hill when frost covered the floorboards of the little house across the road, where they were staying then. "It was between twenty below and forty below for twenty days and nights. By the time I'd get the oil up to the house in the container I was lugging, it was two-thirds gone. The wind would blow it right out in a spume," she laughs, thirty years later.

"Is this really good? Am I really good?"

"All those women at the Bunting—Tillie Olsen, Kay Boyle, Anne Sexton, Maxine Kumin—they were wonderful—they really saved me. The Bunting saved me. It was after Walter died."

"Way back when we were young—Donald Hall, Dick Wilbur. You know, the Old Boys. Look at them now. Is this really okay?" She reads "Translations." "That'll really shock 'em. But nobody will take it. Afraid to touch the stuff. All the guys always worrying about their balls. How do you like that line about the English professor?"

"If you can send one man to the moon why not send them all?" A button she wears on a trip to New York. But takes it off, afraid of offending an old student's new boyfriend.

"What about this one—," she says in Virginia, and reads "Poem for Eight Women." "And here, read this one," and hands me "Ripple Effect."

"Read Delmore Schwartz," she says, "'In Dreams Begin Responsibilities.'" Hopkins, Sexton, Rilke, Ashbery, Grace Paley.

Fresh kale in the garden, green tomatoes. Books by her students, Rosanne Wasserman, Wendy Barker, Kevin Clark.

Driving over the mountain into Middlebury, and back again. Sitting in the car, looking up at stars, talking constellations, bears, telling stories. In the winter, cracking the ice to get water from the stream, carrying buckets, and the wood frozen in a pile out front. Melting snow.

Sometimes her house filled with students passing through. Up for a day or a week or a month. Some leaving a patched roof, others a dog in need of a home, poems to read.

Who's famous? Who's not famous enough? Who got famous too early? Who got famous too late? Who got too famous? Who got famous after she died? Talking about Plath and the horrible Janet Malcolm article, Elizabeth Bishop's "Moose," May Swenson and her humor, their kinship. Talking about language. "Poems come to me through my ear," she says.

"Listen, remember this for the rest of your life: fuck the critics, don't pay any attention to them." Talking about not playing the system.

While Ruth is over the mountain, Bianca and I pick the crabapples. We make baskets out of our shirts and carry the fruit into the kitchen, piling the crabapples up on the kitchen table. Ruth comes home, picks up a plastic bag and fills it with more fruit. We drop the good ones into a silver bowl. Prop up the metal stems with the cheesecloth and set the big pot onto the wood-burning cookstove with its perfect irradiating heat. We boil the glasses for the jelly, cook the fruit, let it drain through the cheesecloth sack, juice dripping into the bowl beneath. And then we boil the juice with sugar, let it roll-boil, add pectin, let it boil again, stirring. We fill the glass jars, wiping the edges, placing the boiled lids on top and setting the jars to jell. Saturday night on Brandon Mountain, in the town of Goshen, in the house of poetry. Ruth Stone labeling the jelly jars in her round, firm script.

"People should always try to read poetry aloud. Listen to the music in this poem. Listen to the way the words fit together." And she picks up Rebecca Seiferle's *The Ripped Out Seam* and reads:

> The toad has the patience of street people,
> derelicts, winos, anyone who lives
> on minuscule realities
> others cannot use. Sometimes as loudly
> dressed as any gangster, he does
> the two-stepped shuffle in mustard-colored
> shoes. . . .

(92)

"Sometimes you've got to shock 'em. Humor's good for that. Make them laugh. They never expect it. They're never prepared for it."

"I first met her in Harvard Yard," says Leslie Fiedler before Ruth gives a poetry reading at the Buffalo Seminary. "I saw a young woman taking zigzagging leaps across the grass. I went up to her and asked if she was okay, if she needed help. She said no. She was fine. She was trying to cross the lawn without stepping on the ants."

I first met Ruth at NYU, in the English Department. She was giving a poetry reading, and everyone was very somber. Except for me and Angela Hodge. We kept laughing at the funny lines. Hooting, really. We kept getting dirty looks from the serious people around us. I memorized "Curtains" afterward. Ruth Stone saved my life. She changed my course. She showed me that poetry can be fully integrated into experience. That is okay. It is a good way to live. If you need to. She showed me that any subject is a fine subject for a poem. She showed what happened when you said the unexpected. Did the unexpected. Exposed the heart entirely, shamelessly.

She said, laughing, "What's the matter, you afraid to be naked in front of everybody?"

"They'll see I'm scum," I said.

"We're all scum," she replied. "And some people are really bad scum: they don't even know they are scum and they kill people and torture people. We're scum too. But we're not that bad."

Poems about family, about homelessness, prostitution, astrophysics, biology, religion, government, illness, the atmosphere, the universe, vegetables, her dead husband, her dying dog, our dying earth. The poetry of Ruth Stone is about truth and it is about love. Stripped down, she tells a story filled with the music of our language. Like Muriel Rukeyser, whose love and rage were wide and great, Ruth is a poet without simple category. A seer, wise woman, poet who heals, feels, listens. Poet of utter originality. Who knows pathos and laughter, terror, loss, and the complexities of love. The outrageous, the passionate, devastation, birth, starvation, molecular breakdown, aeronautic capabilities, porcupines in trees, telescopic vision, magnification. Who writes poems on the backs of envelopes or cereal boxes, fills notebooks. Who has a house on Brandon Mountain whose fibers are poems. Who has rooms of notebooks untouched, poems untyped, enough to fill a dozen thick volumes. Who never stops writing. Who cannot stop writing as she cannot stop feeling, seeing, empathizing, placing history into the present and then the future. Who knows music and tragedy, beauty and humor, despair—but through writing, hope. And questions her own brilliance, attributing light to students, young poets, lesser poets.

Who is herself a great constellation, the finest teacher, who sprung poets from her like Medusa sprung snakes, while all along her own voice offers the scope of seasonal wisdom to any listener, as all the great poets of this world in every age have done. Who loves a great range of voices. Whose voice is entirely distinct. Reflecting the most minute as she reflects what is most terrible and huge. The human condition, the natural world, the universe. She is witness and prophet. Who teaches young poets as she teaches those who read or listen to her poems, crossing the lines of age, class, race. I follow her shadow, moving from poem to poem. As light travels through the solar system, I am here in her brilliance, there in her darkness. And her brilliance is very great. Darkness? A part of my own individual reality, fantasies, histories. Her poems, like helium, rise through her home. "Speak," she says. "Get underneath the easy stuff. You've got to open yourself up to really listen, really hear. And remember your mother. How you felt when you thought she was dying. How her nearly dying changed your life. Made you appreciate things more, see more clearly. Pain can do that. And loss. They let the universe in."

Works Cited

Seiferle, Rebecca. "The Toad." *The Ripped-Out Seam*. Riverdale-on-Hudson, NY: Sheep Meadow, 1993.

4 Like a Laser Beam
Martha Nell Smith

Among Emily Dickinson's additions to or revisions of Jesus' Beatitudes (Matthew 5:3-11; Luke 6:20-26) is "Blessed are they that play" (L 690 to the Norcrosses).[1] Most readers have at least a little sense of play, yet too often the importance of having fun remains undervalued in serious intellectual and/or artistic interrogations. Occasionally, however, a Wise One with a sense of play generous and incisive enough to make us take her or him seriously reveals the significance of comedy and humor, not merely in providing relief, but also in producing new types of intellectual, spiritual, and even physical knowledge. Dickinson herself is one of these poet-prophets, and it is a very special pleasure indeed when her wit and wisdom resonate in one of our contemporaries. Reading Dickinson's Beatitude, few poets immediately come to mind, but Ruth Stone, whose very name evokes delight and profundity, is one whom I always and intimately associate with the Amherst bard's aphorism. Like all great poets, Stone elicits an admiration and appreciation not simply for her work, but also for the world, and its many taken-for-granted pleasures.

Most fitting, then, is the fact that I first heard Ruth Stone read at a Celebration of Emily Dickinson and Contemporary Women's Poetry held in 1986 as one of the centennial commemorations of Dickinson's death. When I was honored by being asked to write this essay on Stone, I immediately thought of that wonderful Friday morning in April nearly a decade ago when I heard Ruth's voice as she read her own and Dickinson's poems. I also recalled a splendid spring morning two years later when I interviewed her at length about being a poet, particularly a woman poet. Those two moments stand out as the most significant to share, for both repeatedly and variously answer the question that serves as the title of Stone's volume *Who Is the Widow's Muse?* On the first occasion, Stone displayed her sense of being a woman poet in America and in a lineage with Dickinson, and on the second she examined her sources of inspiration in grandmothers, great-grandmothers, aunts, mothers, daughters. To tell about each instance, I will closely examine a few poems chosen by Stone as vital for establishing communication and thereby cultivating understanding between and among readers.

Walking into the Celebration, I was greeted by a woman's Hoosier intonations, a distinctive twang that was both mellifluous and craggy and that has not faded in an absorbing, amazing life decades away from the Midwest. Stone's voice wraps itself lovingly around every word, and the first thing I heard her say was the following, about Emily Dickinson:

When I read her poems, these original, hard as steel poems, and I feel the intensity in every word, words used in new ways, bent to her will, then I think she was self-sufficient, an artist whose mind was never asleep, whose concentration recreated, made fresh all that she saw and felt, as though she saw through the ordinary barriers, not as a visionary, but as a laser beam. But when I think of how little recognition she received in her lifetime, and how devastated she must have felt, though her fierce pride concealed it, then I am angry and sad. Yes, a great artist knows and can work in almost total isolation, but it is a terrible thing to have to do. The original mind seems eccentric, even crazy sometimes. In her cryptic inventions, she broke the tiresome mold of American poetry. We still stand among those shards and splinters.

Some say that people write their autobiographies in the characteristics they notice in others, and Stone might just as well have been speaking of herself as of Dickinson. Stone's poems are strong; they, as Dickinson said of her beloved sister-in-law Susan Huntington Gilbert Dickinson's way with words, "need no prop to stand" (L 722).

In fact, Stone's poems hold up to almost everything. Intense, deceptively artless, original, provocative, moving, the simplest, most-taken-for-granted words are transformative when bent to

Stone's will, demanding that readers awaken to life's breathtaking intensity, always available yet too rarely savored. Stone pares language so that it cuts right to essence, to the bone as it were. Thus she appreciates Dickinson's economical refusal to use words as dross, and her laserbeam metaphor echoes Susan's obituary characterizing Emily's linguistic wit as a "Damascus blade gleaming and glancing in the sun." In many of her remarks about Emily, Susan might just as well have been writing of Ruth Stone:

Like a magician she caught the shadowy apparitions of her brain and tossed them in startling picturesqueness to her friends, who, charmed with their simplicity and homeliness as well as profundity, fretted that she had so easily made palpable the tantalizing fancies forever eluding their bungling, fettered grasp. . . . With no creed, no formalized faith, hardly knowing the names of dogmas, she walked this life with the gentleness and reverence of old saints, with the firm step of martyrs who sing while they suffer.

Like her predecessor Dickinson, Stone is an astonishing verbal acrobat whose skills are intended to communicate and to say the world as she sees it. And that Stone has known great suffering makes her, as it did Dickinson, tremendously empathetic and acutely sensitive but never self-pitying.

When Stone read some of Dickinson's poems, she did not comment upon them but simply read one after another. The four she chose focus on language's powers and powerful emotion, and the poem with which she began encapsulates the monumental affectiveness of each that can completely transform perception and experience:

> Many a phrase has the
> English language –
> I have heard but one –
> Low as the laughter of the
> Cricket,
> Loud, as the Thunder's Tongue –
>
> Murmuring, like old Caspian
> Choirs,
> When the Tide's a'lull –
> Saying itself in new inflection –
> Like a Whipporwil –

Breaking in bright Orthography
On my simple sleep –
Thundering it's Prospective –
Till I stir, and weep –

Not for the Sorrow, done me –
But the push of Joy –
Say it again, Saxon!
Hush – Only to me!

(F 12; P 276)

The "one" phrase Dickinson hears anthropomorphizes nature's noises, both of the smallest creatures and the most gargantuan events, imbuing an insect with glee and a storm with speech. Four decades ago, Rebecca Patterson argued that the one phrase was Dickinson's rapturous "I love you" for another woman. Indeed, the phrase comforts like the soothing, predictable chorus of a regular, peaceful tide, lifts one to a kind of ecstasy in which, as Robert Frost would reiterate, "never again would birds' song be the same" (Lathem and Thompson 451), and makes even of one's dreams a sense that Dickinson compares to an illuminating form of spelling the world, of rendering experience in the illusion of order we call language. All of these responses that free one for such play with quotidian events evoke a spell like that cast by the exhilaration of being in love, an Edenic state in which all is seen, heard, felt anew.

For Stone, as well as for Dickinson, poetry and love "coeval come" (P 1247), and Stone read three poems that might be about love (or its loss) or that might be about the fate of Dickinson's poetry: "When I hoped, I recollect" (F 23; P 768), "The Loneliness One dare not sound" (F 39; P 777), and "One Anguish – in a Crowd" (F 28; P 565). The last lines of Dickinson that Stone read—that poetry, that "Repealless thing," is "impotent to end – When once it has begun"—iterate the stunning confidence of an artist who knows she has created poems demanded by posterity but who does not know how they will find their way. Concluding her reading of her forerunner's poems, Stone remarked, "What I'm most struck by in Emily Dickinson is her amazing use of language. She felt very keenly the lack of recognition in her own life—her consummately beautiful poetry was so advanced. She was a child of the future, and it was lonely to be that way."

Also a child of the future, Ruth Stone knows how lonely being the bearer of such foresight can be. Yet fortunately for us, she has used even her experience of loneliness to make connections, both to predecessors such as Dickinson who have taught her and to readers like us whom she teaches. Some of those connections are through hilarious commentaries that make us take delight in the most mundane of the everyday, such as "The Nose," perpetually overlooked by each of us:

> Everyone complains about the nose.
> If you notice, it is stuck to your face.
> In the morning it will be red.
> If you are a woman you can cover it with makeup.
> If you are a man it means you had a good time last night.
> Noses are phallic symbols.
> So are fingers, monuments, trees, and cucumbers.
> The familiar, "He knows his stuff," should be looked into.
> There is big business in nose jobs,
> The small nose having gained popularity during the Christian
>   boom. . . .
>
> (*S-HC* 83)

Stone knows how to have fun and knows how important sharing her wry, comic view of the world is. After all, the ability to laugh at ourselves and at the world we have made is one of the key elements necessary for personal, social, cultural change. Such capacity for humor is also a necessary complement to the ability to plumb seemingly unfathomable emotions, such as the grief and anger at a beloved husband who took his own life, an event Stone explores in "Codicil," "Habit," "Curtains," and "Turn Your Eyes Away," all in *Second-Hand Coat*.

Stone told me that she did not know if "Turn Your Eyes Away" was a difficult poem to write. "It just came," she said, after her husband Walter had been dead twenty-four, twenty-five years. "It had taken that long. Some poems are on the surface, while some are not there at all, but all poetry is about making significant connections, connections that are always different, always coming out in different facets. Truth cannot be exposed except in bits and pieces." The wise poet both looks and, as in the case of "Turn Your Eyes Away," waits for connections to be made.

Extraordinarily conscious of connections and disconnections, Stone has extensively examined problems of literary creativity for women who have traditionally been disjoined from a literary heritage and from language itself. As Stone's looking back to Emily Dickinson and the extensive recuperation projects in criticism, anthologies, and new editions of women's writings testify, we are at the advent of a renaissance for women writers, and a literary heritage for women is being delineated and/or restored. Yet as Stone and critics such as Sandra Gilbert and Susan Gubar remind us, the "linguistic problem" for "female self-signification" is much more basic than women writers being erased from literary history (Gilbert and Gubar 25). Stone muses on "Names":

> My grandmother's name was Nora Swan.
> Old Aden Swan was her father. But who was her mother?
> I don't know my great-grandmother's name.
> I don't know how many children she bore.
> Like rings of a tree the years of woman's fertility.
> Who were my great-aunt Swans?
> For every year a child; diphtheria, dropsy, typhoid.
> Who can bother naming all those women churning butter,
> leaning on scrub boards, holding to iron bedposts
> sweating in labor? My grandmother knew the names
> of all the plants on the mountain. Those were the names
> she spoke of to me. Sorrel, lamb's ear, spleenwort, heal-all;
> never go hungry, she said, when you can gather a pot of
>   greens.
> She had a finely drawn head under a smooth cap of hair
> pulled back to a bun. Her deep-set eyes were quick to notice
> in love and anger. Who are the women who nurtured her for
>   me?
> Who handed her in swaddling flannel to my great-grandmoth-
>   er's breast?
> Who are the women who brought my great-grandmother tea
> and straightened her bed? As anemone in midsummer, the air
> cannot find them and grandmother's been at rest for forty
>   years.

In me are all the names I can remember—pennyroyal,
   boneset,
bedstraw, toadflax—from whom I did descend in perpetuity.
                                                    (*S-HC* 23)

As Gilbert and Gubar point out, Stone refuses merely to accept the linguistic mortality to which patriarchal customs of naming resign women and "dreams of an archaic language that predates the patronymics of culture." What she recovers are "names of power, regal autographs drawn from a feminized nature" (25). Through these she makes connections to her female ancestors, connections that would otherwise be lost through convention's erasures.

In her poetry, Stone repeatedly makes those vital connections to women, and in our interview she talked about the importance of her "reclamation of a maternal legacy," about her great-grandmother writing poetry, her grandmother painting and writing poems and a novel, and her mother reading Tennyson aloud while Stone was "at her breast" and "singing all the time." Throughout her career, Stone has emphasized the importance of such women to her artistic vision. "How to Catch Aunt Harriette" reflects upon the influence of a beloved aunt, older by four years than Stone, who was a wonderful storyteller and with whom Stone used to play private games:

> Mary Cassatt has her in a striped dress with a
> child on her lap, the child's foot in a wash basin.
> Or Charlotte Mew speaks in her voice of the feeling
> that comes at evening with home-cawing rooks.
> Or Aunt Harriette sometimes makes an ineffable
> gesture between the lines of Trollope.
> In Indianapolis, together we rode the belching city bus to
> high school. It was my first year, she was a senior. We were
> nauseated every day by the fumes, by the unbearable
> streets. Aunt Harriette was the last issue of my
> Victorian grandparents. Once after school she
> invited me to go with her to Verner's.
> What was *Verner's*? I didn't ask and Aunt Harriette didn't say.
> We walked three miles down manicured Meridian.
> My heels rubbed to soft blisters. Entering an empty
> wood-echoing room fronting the sidewalk,
> we sat at a plain plank table and Aunt Harriette

> ordered two glasses of iced ginger ale.
> The varnish of light on Aunt Harriette
> had the quality of a small eighteenth-century
> Dutch painting. My tongue with all its buds intact
> slipped in the amber sting. It was my first hint
> of the connoisseur, an induction rarely repeated;
> yet so bizarre, so beyond me,
> that I planned my entire life from its indications.
>
> (*S-HC* 5)

Aunt Harriette offered Stone a new taste of life, cultivated a previously unknown appreciation in her, and the memory of that initiation bathes the poet in consciousness of women artists and writers gone before.

The inspiration Stone takes from her female progenitors is various. Aunt Harriette's world was one of exploration, storytelling, daily mystery, and adventure. Yet her frustrated Aunt Maud's example also proved to be a profound teacher, as Stone examines in "How Aunt Maud Took to Being a Woman":

> A long hill sloped down to Aunt Maud's brick house.
> You could climb an open stairway up the back
> to a plank landing where she kept her crocks of wine.
> I got sick on stolen angelfood cake and green wine
> and slept in her feather bed for a week.
> Nobody said a word. Aunt Maud just shifted
> the bottles. Aunt's closets were all cedar lined.
> She used the same pattern for her house dresses—
> thirty years. Plain ugly, closets full of them,
> you could generally find a new one cut and laid
> out on her sewing machine. She preserved,
> she canned. Her jars climbed the basement walls.
> She was a vengeful housekeeper. She kept the blinds
> pulled down in the parlor. Nobody really walked
> on her hardwood floors. You lived in the kitchen.
> Uncle Cal spent a lot of time on the back porch
> waiting to be let in.
>
> (*S-HC* 32)

Her creative energies wasted on a rage for household order, her imagination stifled into making wonderful wine, Aunt Maud exhausts herself on the trappings of life while life itself eludes her.

By taking her as a poetic subject, Stone underscores the fact that poetry and love, poetry and life coeval come. A poet is not removed from life but teaches us aesthetic appreciation for the rough and tumble, the haphazard, the grit of living far from Maud's manic order spelling a powerful vitality contained. A poet teaches us to "dwell in" life's, in imagination's "Possibility" (F 22; P 657). As have countless women and countless generations of women, Maud's living and art are constricted by her having been marked as a woman and for women's roles. Efficiency, polish, preservation, and precise patterns supplant spark, spontaneity, the trial and error of intuition, and the inevitable spills of unpredictability as Maud's anger makes a mausoleum-like museum of her household where she shields the parlor from sunlight and the hardwood floors from footfalls. Aunt Maud's house is like verse that wants to be poetry but that has removed itself from the messiness, the contradictions, the confusions (in Frost's words, the real "stuff") of life.

Dickinson, Aunt Maud, Aunt Harriette. They are all muses for Ruth Stone. In a culture where women have served as the passive inspirational objects for men, the muse has long been recognized as problematic for a woman writer. The analogies traditionally drawn between creative production and reproduction privilege the male creator and heteropatriarchy and romanticize the poetic process itself. Yet in *Who Is the Widow's Muse?* Stone interrogates the very notion of the muses and, like a laser beam, cuts through many an obfuscating myth about the sources of creativity.

The fifty-two poems of the *Widow's Muse* cycle are prefaced by "All Time Is Past Time":

> Goliath is struck by the stone.
> The stone turns into a bird.
> The bird sings in her window.
> Time is absurd. It flows backward.
> It is married to the word.
>
> This is the window of the giant's eyes.
> This is the bird singing alone.
> This is the river of forgetting.
> This is the chosen stone.
> This is Goliath's widow.

Struck by the stone he leaps
into the future. He lies
a monolith, a rune, light
from a distant nova. Not even a bone
remembers begetting him ever.

The song is a monotone.
She is the word and the window.
She is the stone and the bird.
She is the bed of the river.

                                    (*WM* prologue)

Judeo-Christian mythology remembers that the boy David slew the
giant Goliath but does not remark upon Goliath's widow. Monolithic, these stories lie, excising as they do the experiences of half
of humankind or at best relegating their mention to footnotes and
appendices. Unmarried, the widow sings stories marked as "special
interest" and thereby labeled "minor." Yet as the poet puns on her
surname in her closing couple of lines, she reminds us that the river,
biblically a symbol for new life, is embedded and gushes forth from
the life's songs such as that of the widow.

The poems of *Who Is the Widow's Muse?*, which mark each week
in an annual cycle of mourning, catalog a vast variety of mostly
unconventional candidates for the muse: crow, trash-can, x-ray vision, the deceased husband, "a char woman with a hangover" (*WM*
7), ice cream, the widow herself, a simple dinner of "lentils / and
carrots and onions" (11), her "dead mother" (12), the fantasy of
being a frog, "the inexorable / law of death" (14), her car named
"Violet Hunt" (15), "fetish? . . . footwear?" (16), expectation, "all
the women of the world" (22), a key to a scented cedar box, a
shopping cart, an amoeba, a city pigeon, "the dangerous / highway
and empty corridors" (54). Does the muse dwell in the bladder?
the linen closet? Could she be "effervescent" (41)? Was she once a
"marble statue" now "painfully shattered" (31)? Is she "carnal? Could
she have hot pants" (33)? Could she be envious of two teenaged
girls sighted from a passing bus, girls she christens Eve and Helen,
after women perpetually degraded by the unreconstructed stories of
Western mythologies? Who was Maude Gonne's (Yeats's sometime

muse) muse, anyway? The muse notices that many of the working girls of the Utica cotton mills are "sending their brothers to college" and "sighs." " 'The widow's muse / certainly lives in Eden,' / the widow said" (43). And, as Dickinson realized, Eden is not some superhuman site but, integral to life itself, is "always eligible" (L 391). And of life?:

> She realizes that life
> exists in minute details,
> packets of energy,
> the signal moment of awakening.
>
> (*WM* 52)

Via this sequence, the widow's eyes are opened so that she sees poetic possibility in everything, and that is the "key."

Though she is a full professor at SUNY at Binghamton, Ruth Stone considers her house in Vermont, purchased by a Kenyon fellowship and repaired by a Shelley award and a Guggenheim—"nothing but poetry has gone into that house"—home:

> "Vermont is a Greek island," the widow says.
> The widow's muse wraps her head in a veil.
> "Basta, basta," the muse cries,
> "you begin to understand!"
>
> (*WM* 55)

Thus Stone harkens back to the Greek lesbian poet Sappho whose person and place of being have provided women poets with a metaphor for the isolation (not to be confused with loneliness) necessary for creation. "Isolation? I can make isolation wherever I am—on a bus, a train, in a waiting room, anywhere," Stone told me during our interview. "I once wrote a story that was published in *Commentary* with my foot against the door, typewriter on my lap, kids on the other side of the door. It's the only time I ever acted that way." The muse is no idealized figure. The muse is, as Stone's fifty-two poems in *Widow's Muse* make clear, an unflinching, diligent, persistent writing habit. Poetry springs from bold confrontation and acceptance of the facts of life:

The muse shakes her head.
"No. We must get back to the real thing.
The blood and meat of the world."
The muse took the widow in her arms.
"Now say it with me," the muse said.
"Once and for all. . .he is forever dead."

(*WM* 59)

Ruth Stone's muses are real, the blood, the meat of the world. Refusing to romanticize the creative process, she exhorts us with a delightful profundity that embraces her world and her relationships with a clear-eyed, demystified sense of appreciative wonder. When we began our interview and were talking of poetry and song, she reminded us that not only are muses forerunners, but that indeed even a small child shall lead them. Saying, "I used to make up all the songs I sang to my children," Stone suddenly began singing, in a beautiful clean voice I wish all could hear:

I have three daughters
Like greengage plums,
Sitting all day
And sighing all day
And sucking their thumbs;
Singing, Mama won't you fetch and carry,
And Daddy, won't you let us marry,
Singing, sprinkle snow down on Mama's hair
And lordy, give us our share.

(*S-HC* 110)

May we all, like "Alexander Mehielovitch Touritzen" (*S-HC* 55) be exonerated. May we be forgiven. May we rise with the angels as we spread wide our "narrow Hands / To gather Paradise" (P 657) from the quotidian experience transformed by poetry.

Thank you, Ruth—my mother, sister, spiritual lover, friend.

Note

1. Dickinson's poems (P) and letters (L) are quoted from Thomas H. Johnson's editions and will use the number assigned by Johnson. References to poems in R. W. Franklin's edition of the fascicles (F) will give the fascicle number only.

Works Cited

Dickinson, Susan Huntington Gilbert. "Miss Emily Dickinson of Amherst." Obituary in *Springfield Republican* 18 May 1886. Box 9. Dickinson Papers. Houghton Library, Harvard University, Cambridge.

Franklin, R. W., ed. *The Manuscript Books of Emily Dickinson*. Cambridge, MA: Belknap, 1981.

Gilbert, Sandra Caruso Mortola, and Susan Dreyfuss David Gubar. "Ceremonies of the Alphabet: Female Grandmatologies and the Female Autograph." *The Female Autograph: Theory and Practice of Autobiography from the Tenth to the Twentieth Century*. Ed. Donna Stanton. Chicago and London: U of Chicago P, 1984. 21–48.

Johnson, Thomas H., ed. *The Poems of Emily Dickinson*. 3 vols. Cambridge, MA: Belknap, 1955.

Johnson, Thomas H., and Theodora Ward, eds. *The Letters of Emily Dickinson*. 3 vols. Cambridge, MA: Belknap, 1958.

Lathem, Edward C., and Lawrance Thompson, eds. *Robert Frost: Poetry and Prose*. New York: Holt, 1972.

Part II   *A Life of Art*

I listen in the dark
to the bowed strings of sadness and pain.

—Ruth Stone, *"Liebeslied"*

5 Mapping Ruth Stone's Life and Art
Wendy Barker

Tillie Olsen, in the *Iowa Review* collection *Extended Outlooks*, calls Ruth Stone "one of the major poets" of the latter twentieth century, describing her poetic voice as "clear, pure, fierce" (Gilbert et al. 327). She is not alone in her high praise for this poet; numerous other prominent writers have lauded Stone's poetry: Patricia Blake in *Time* singles out Ruth Stone as one of the most powerful and sensuous of woman poets writing since Sappho (85). Sandra M. Gilbert praises the "terrible clarity of her vision" (Gilbert et al. 325), and Julie Fay in the *Women's Review of Books* insists that a place be made for Stone "among the better-known poets of [her] generation" (18). Frances Mayes, reviewing Stone's collection *Second-Hand Coat* in the *San Jose Mercury News*, observes that Stone is not only "wise and abundantly gifted," but that, in addition, her poetry is "stunning work" that spans a "superb range of evocative experience" (24).

Perhaps it is, in fact, her poetry's dazzling range of experience that, paradoxically, has caused the work of Ruth Stone only recently to be given the attention it deserves. For the work of Stone is as difficult to categorize as the poetry of Emily Dickinson. Whereas Donald Hall has described Stone's work in *Hungry Mind Review* as "relentless as a Russian's" (3), her poems are also lush, lyrical, even at times Tennysonian in their music and meter. With half a dozen collections of her poetry, and with her poems anthologized in over twenty collections, it is high time we begin to try to understand Ruth Stone's virtuosity.

Born 8 June 1915 in Roanoke, Virginia, in her grandparents' house, Ruth Perkins Stone was surrounded by relatives who wrote poetry, painted, practiced law, and taught school. Intrigued by the large collection of books in her grandparents' library, Stone began reading at three. She attended kindergarten and first grade in Roanoke, but then moved to Indianapolis where she lived with her father's parents. Living at that time in her paternal grandparents' home in Indianapolis was Stone's Aunt Harriette, who delighted in playing writing and drawing games with her niece. Together they wrote poems and drew comical cartoons: Ruth Stone has said that Aunt Harriette was the best playmate she ever had. The poet's mother, Ruth Ferguson Perkins, also encouraged her daughter's "play." For her, too, poetry was an essential ingredient of life: while nursing Ruth as a baby, she read the works of Tennyson out loud. And as her child grew, she openly delighted in her daughter's irrepressible creativity.

Writing, poetry, drawing, and music surrounded the young poet while she grew up in Indianapolis. Her father—Roger McDowell Perkins—was a drummer, who often practiced at home. As Stone tells it, on the nights he was not gambling, he would bring home an elegant box of the best chocolates and some new classical records. There would be music and candy and he would read out loud to them, sometimes from the Bible, sometimes from humorous pieces by Bill Nye. He was "crazy about funny stuff," says Stone.[1] "Funny stuff" was, in fact, a large part of the pattern of family life in Indianapolis. The poet remembers her uncles at dinner parties who told one fascinating story after another, convulsing the family with their humor. Every member of her father's family had an extraordinary sense of the ridiculous—they saw right through the superficial.

And yet, this family of English descent also played its part in polite Indianapolis society. The poet's paternal grandfather was a senator, and in keeping with the familial social position, his wife gave frequent formal tea parties. Stone remembers pouring tea, learning to be a lady—something, she says, she later "had to learn to forget."

Perhaps, in fact, part of the fascination of Stone's poetry has to do with the counterpoint between a lyrical, ladylike gentility and a sharp, blunt, even bawdy ability to see into the hard core of experience. For the poetry of Ruth Stone is as informed by a knowledge of contemporary science as it is by a novelist's eye for character, an artist's eye for color, a musician's ear for sound. At the age of eight, Ruth Stone read about meteors. In the grassy yard at night, she would lie on her back and study the stars. Once she found in the library a photograph of a galaxy that, as she puts it, "changed me terribly." And when, at eleven, she read in *The American Scholar* about the new theory of the expanding universe, she became inquisitive about physics. She was also passionate about botany: "I wanted to absorb everything about the real world." When not intensely observing "real" phonomena, she read everything she could find; frequently, she took encyclopedias and dictionaries to bed with her. She was, as she puts it, "just obsessive about language."

It is no wonder, then, with such intense and diverse interests, that this poet's complex work has defied easy categorization. In a paper delivered at the 1988 MLA Convention, Diane Wakoski recognized Stone's poetry as embodying the comedic tradition of Dante, with its enormous range of human experience. As Wakoski puts it in her chapter in this volume, "Ruth Stone is a poet opening the door to an American comedic verse." Stone's work can also be compared to Shakespeare's in that, immersed in the world of her poems, we find ourselves moving inexplicably from laughter to tears and back to laughter again, shaking in response to something larger than humor, than grief, something of the two, and more. Reading Ruth Stone's poetry is like sitting on a summer lawn at night, engulfed in the scent of jasmine, and suddenly the night sky cracks open, a meteor slices through—and at the same time, someone is telling you the funniest joke you have ever heard.

In an Iridescent Time, Stone's first book collection, published in 1959, includes poems written primarily while the poet's husband, novelist and poet Walter Stone, was still alive, teaching at Vassar College. The Stones had three children by that time—Marcia, born in 1942, Phoebe, born in 1949, and Abigail, born in 1953. By 1960, Ruth Stone's reputation was already established: in 1955 she won the Kenyon Review Fellowship in Poetry, received the Bess Hokin prize from *Poetry*, and had recorded her poems at the Library of Congress. Individual poems had been published in the best magazines, including *Kenyon Review*, *Poetry*, the *New Yorker*, and *Partisan Review*.

This first book collection is aptly named: poems here are indeed "iridescent"; in fact, they shimmer with music, at times with echoes of Tennyson and the romantics. These poems focus upon youthful, exuberant family life, as in the title poem, "In an Iridescent Time," in which the speaker remembers her own mother, washing and hanging out to dry the brilliantly colored "fluttering intimacies of life." The laundry in this poem shines in memory, gleams with the energy of the daughters who hone "their knuckles" on the washboard (*IT* 7).

The poem "In an Iridescent Time" is also characteristic of much of this volume in its formal qualities: "tub" rhymes with "rub-adub," and the girls shake the clothes "from the baskets two by two," draping them "Between the lilac bushes and the yew: Brown gingham, pink, and skirts of Alice blue" (7). The vitality and whimsy of this collection spring from the opening poem of the volume, "When Wishes Were Fishes." Here the rhythm and meter gallop, rollicking along with "All that clapping and smacking of gulls, / And that slapping of tide on rock," when "Our senses twanged on the sea's gut string, / . . . and the young ladies in a flock / . . . ran the soprano scale and jumped the waves in a ring." Here the air is "sun-charged" by the "kelp-smelling sea," at "the edge of the world and free" (1).

And yet this shimmering world is not entirely free, not only youthful and buoyant. Throughout this first collection, in fact, a hint of an undertow surfaces. The "Sunday wish" of the girls in "When Wishes Were Fishes" is "to bottle a dredged-up jellyfish"; innocents, they are also aware of the "Seaweed and dead fish" strewn on the sand (1). Even in this first volume, the sense of vitality is underscored by a sense that all this lushness, this youth, cannot last, that something more, ominous, is lurking close at hand.

"The Pear," for instance, with a "tallow rump slow rounded, a pelt thin," eventually will be dried by the "husbandman" for her "pits" (47). Lush, lovely, and funny, the poem is also wryly grim.

As the poet says in "An Old Song," "Now the fat's gone, some gnaw the bone with me. / I tell you death's hard fought for, hard to kill" (45). "For a Photograph of My Mother at the Beach" eulogizes the "dead white ladies" who "dance / In spanking striped beach garments"; the poet's tears for the memory of her mother and for the past are compared to the oyster's pearls—but are as "wasted as ocean weirs" (40).

The poet's second volume of poetry, *Topography*, maps the territory of grief at its sharpest, its most acute. If *In an Iridescent Time* maps a country of summer backyards suffused with sweet memory, then *Topography* charts the moment of the meteor's direct hit, the moment of the wound, the gash. Written after the sudden suicide of the poet's husband, Walter Stone, which occurred while the family lived in England, *Topography* was not published until eleven years after her first book, in 1970. In this second volume, the music is still there, but reliance upon end rhyme lessens, form opens, as nothing, not even the striking, frighteningly honest images of these poems, can contain the poet's grief.

The poems that comprise *Topography* were for the most part not written until the years 1963-1965, when the poet was a fellow of the Radcliffe Institute. This second collection opens with a short poem reflecting on marriage, "Dream of Light in the Shade":

> Now that I am married I spend
> My hours thinking about my husband.
> I wind myself about his shelter.
>
> *(TOP* 3)

As if an echo from *In an Iridescent Time*, this poem, with its light touch, its wry attitude toward a wife's centering her life around her mate, causes the rest of the volume to be read even more tragically, since the central fact underlying the book is that there is no longer anything to wind around, no longer any center, any firm ground.

In the second poem of *Topography*, "Arrivals and Departures," "The terminal echoes in the ears of a single traveler, / Meaningless as the rumble of the universe" (7). *Topography* charts the journey from that arrival at the place of death, that departure from "normal"

life that the death of the mate initiated. It is as if the poet has been
dropped off in this meaningless, rumbling "terminal" and must
now map out her destination, her itinerary, alone.

Imagery in this poem is stark, ugly; the counter in the terminal
is wiped with a "grey rag," the coffee bar is dirty. Everything has
been spoiled, dirtied, decayed by death: "It is so difficult to look
at the deprived, or smell their decay, / But now I am among them.
I too, am a leper, a warning" (14). Poems in this collection contain
images of "sucked-down refuse" (10), "dead still fog" (11), "repelling
flesh" (12).

And yet, under the decay, under the almost devastating shock,
the poems also trace the way out of this "terminal." One way is
through the brutal honesty of many of these poems: "Denouement,"
for instance, surveys the territory of anger following the death of
this husband who took his own life: "After many years I knew who
it was who had died. / Murderer, I whispered, you tricked me"
(17). But it is not only anger that is so honestly, powerfully mapped
in these poems. In "Stasis," the poet says, "I wait for the touch of
a miracle" (21). And gradually, through the pages of *Topography*,
small miracles do occur. Slow healing is the subject of such poems
as "Reaching Out":

> We hear the sound of a hammer in the pony shed,
> And the clean slap of linens drying in the sun;
> Climbing the grass path,
> Reaching out before we are there
> To know, nothing is changed.
>
> *(TOP* 31)

Old memories begin to surface, shining into the present time like
those in *In an Iridescent Time*, as in "Green Apples":

> In August we carried the old horsehair mattress
> To the back porch
> And slept with our children in a row.
> . . . .
> I was happy.
>
> *(TOP* 37)

But for all its moments of "stasis," of acceptance, even at times
of brief happiness beyond the grief, *Topography* charts no simple

country. Section 4, for instance, moves beyond human experience to draw upon the natural world and shows Stone's brilliance as a naturalist. In poems such as the very funny "Pig Game," in which pigs, like poets, "live within / And scan without" (48), and the determined "Habitat," in which the wolverine "is built for endurance" (49), the poet moves beyond the shock and anger of early grief to a sense of wide perspective, humor, and rich connections.

Topography provides a plan of survival: like the wolverine of "Habitat," who "knows her own parcel" of territory "by the singular smell of her feces," the poet has mapped her "parcel" (49). It is a parcel that also includes enormous comic elements, especially in the nursery-rhyme-like poems such as "I Have Three Daughters." The collection ends with the title poem, "Topography." Funny, wry as the opening poem about marriage, this time, the poet says, "Yes, I remember the turning and holding, / The heavy geography; but map me again, Columbus" (116).

Stone's third book, *Cheap*, is characterized by a physical sense of movement beyond the terminal, beyond the paralysis that underlies much of *Topography*. These poems were in fact written while the poet was migrating from university to university, including the University of Illinois, Indiana University at Bloomington, and the University of California at Davis. That we have moved into an entirely different country from that of *In an Iridescent Time* is clear simply from titles of poems. In Stone's first book, poems are titled "Snow," "Ballet," "Collage," "Swans." In *Cheap*, poems have titles like "Cocks and Mares," "Who's Out," "The Nose," "Bazook," "Bored on a Greyhound," and the much-anthologized concluding title of the volume, "The Song of Absinthe Granny."

In her third collection, the humor of this complex and versatile poet comes into its own. If *Topography* was less mannered, less lyrical (and less ladylike) than *In an Iridescent Time*, *Cheap* is even less so. With this book, the poet has moved through the country of grief and has emerged, seeing everything, right down to its frightening, funny, and devastating core.

The country traveled through in *Cheap* involves even stronger connections between human and nonhuman life than we saw in *Topography*. In "Vegetables I" the eggplants are compared to decapi-

tated human heads "utterly drained of blood." In the market, they
seem

> to be smiling
> In a shy embarrassed manner,
> jostling among themselves.

(*C* 32)

In "Vegetables II,"

> It is the cutting room, the kitchen,
> Where I go like an addict
> To eat of death.
> The eggplant is silent.
> We put our heads together.
> You are so smooth and cool and purple,
> I say. Which of us will it be?

(*C* 33)

Such wryness and pithiness are characteristic of this third collection,
which is tighter, more ironic, and wiser than either of the first two.

And yet the countries charted in the first two volumes are still
present, as themes and styles continue. In the title poem, young
love is the subject of fond scorn: "He was young and cheap . . . I
was easy in my sleep," the two "Braying, galloping / Like a pair of
mules" running "blind as moles" (7). Marriage and the betrayal of
the beloved's death continue as themes. In "Codicil," the poet writes
of a widowed landlady who kept all the eggs her ornithologist
husband collected, comparing all the "secret muted shapes" of "unborn wizened eggs" (9) to the stillborn possibilities for her own
marriage. Unhatched eggs, filed in drawers, are all that's left. In
poems such as "Loss" ("I hid sometimes in the closet among my
own clothes" [10]), "Habit" ("Every day I dig you up. . . . / I show
you my old shy breasts" [15]), and "The Innocent" ("I remember
you / in the sound of an oak stake / Hammered into the frozen heart
of the ground" [16]), the poet continues to examine the country of
widowhood.

Other poems are lighter: "Tic Tac Toe" makes fun of all good
intentions, of people "pulling in their stomachs and promising /

To exercise more, drink less, grow brilliant" (25). A number of the poems in *Cheap* also use the nursery rhyme style of earlier poems. "Bargain," "The Tree," and perhaps most famously "The Song of Absinthe Granny" all incorporate the singsong rhythm of a jingle or a nursery rhyme. Diana O'Hehir observes in her chapter in this volume that Stone's use of rhythms and comical word patterns, coupled with the often terrifying matter of her poems' subjects, accounts for their power. As O'Hehir puts it, Stone "lures the reader in with the familiar rhythms of childhood, promises a pattern that the reader can join in on and follow along with, and then yanks the entire structure out from under the feet" so that the reader is "surprised, startled, and made to follow gasping."

It is also through her use of rapid, unexpected associative leaps that many of the poems in *Cheap* achieve their brilliance. In "Dream of Wild Birds," for instance, the scene is "a movie, a film, a picture, a little frame"; the birds are seen as through x-ray, the flock is described in ballet terms, as

> Meanwhile, the ovum is swelling
> And the sperm is growing agitated. The time for leaving
> The dark blood has come.
>
> (*C* 31)

This volume, with its wry understanding of life in all its guises, is more direct, piercing than either of Stone's previous two collections.

With the publication in 1987 of *Second-Hand Coat: Poems New and Selected*, we find the poet writing in her full power, relying upon a craft, music, wisdom, and humor that knock us over. Here, comedic territory is fully mapped and charted. "Orange Poem Praising Brown" captures the anxieties of the writer (particularly the female writer) with more wit than anything I have ever read: "The quick poem jumped over the lazy woman. / There it goes flapping like an orange with peeling wings" (*S-HC* 29). The dialogue continues between the anxious woman and the brown poem: "Watch it, the poem cries. You aren't wearing any pants / . . . Praise my loose hung dangle, he said. / Tell me about myself in oral fragments" (29). Similarly, "Some Things You'll Need to Know Before You Join the Union" is another comic poem for poets:

> At the poetry factory
> body poems are writing and bleeding.
> . . . .
> The antiwar and human rights poems
> are processed in the white room.
> . . . .
> These poems go for a lot.
> No one wants to mess up.
> There's expensive equipment involved,
> The workers have to be heavy,
> very heavy.
> These poems are packaged in cement.
> You frequently hear them drop with a dull thud.
>
> (*S-HC* 49)

Not a poem in this collection drops with a thud.

Part of *Second-Hand Coat*'s humor has to do with the characters who populate it, characters who remind us of Fred and Ida of "Bazook" in *Cheap*. Dickens-like, Mark Twain-like, and, as Diane Wakoski has said, Booth-cartoon-like, the characters in these poems are outrageously funny—and very real. As Kevin Clark observes in his chapter in this volume, they are often grotesques, in which we recognize ourselves. As in the poem "Bazook," many of these characters have gone "berserk"; yet, as we read, we begin to question, like Emily Dickinson, which madness is sanity, who are the sane, and who the insane. Mrs. Dubosky in "What Can You Do?," Aunt Virginia in "Curtains," Uncle and Little Ivan and Aunt Bess in "The Miracle," the Masons in "Sunday," are all a little daft— and yet, as Kevin Clark notes, are not only funny but are also true, and in their absolute truth show *us* the truth of ourselves.

The humor of *Second-Hand Coat* also extends to the poems that show Stone as an avid student of contemporary science. Just as the young Ruth took encyclopedias to bed with her, the mature Stone reads everything she can about biology, astronomy, physics, the body, the galaxy, neurons, protons. Much of the effect of these poems has to do with her knowledge of the way the world actually works, and in many of these poems, she fuses the wacky humor and drummer's rhythms of her father, the lyricism of her mother's Tennyson, and her own relentless curiosity, wit, and wisdom. "The bunya-bunya is a great louse that sucks," begins "From the Arboretum," a poem that goes on to show the intricacy of relatedness:

> Rings of ants, bark beetles, sponge molds,
> even cockroaches communicate in its armpits.
> But it protests only with the voices of starlings,
> their colony at its top in the forward brush.
> To them it is only an old armchair, a brothel, the front porch.
>
> (*S-HC* 17)

Other poems are even more obviously based upon the poet's scientific knowledge: "Moving Right Along" begins,

> At the molecular level,
> in another dimension,
> oy, are you different!
> That's where it all shreds
> like Watergate.
>
> (*S-HC* 10)

Like the new physicists, who came to the conclusion that pure objectivity cannot exist, Stone questions the possibilities for clear answers in "At the Center":

> The center is simple, they say.
> They say at the Fermi accelerator,
> "Rejoice. A clear and clean
> explanation of matter is possible."

The poem continues with the poet's questioning

> . . . . Where is this place,
> the center they speak of? Currants,
> red as faraway suns, burn on the currant bush.

And the eyes of the beloved, now long dead, are "far underground," where they

> . . . . fall apart,
> while their particles still shoot like meteors
> through space making their own isolated trajectories.
>
> (*S-HC* 3)

In *Second-Hand Coat* this grief of the widow is softened, muted. In "Curtains," another comic-tragic poem, the poet asks at the end,

"See what you miss by being dead?" (15). In "Winter," she asks, "Am I going toward you or away from you on this train?" (18). And in "Message from Your Toes," which begins

> Even in the absence of light
> there is light. Even in the least electron
> there are photons.
> So in a larger sense you must consider your own toes

the poet connects electron, photon, and the toes of the dead husband in a poem that elicits laughter in the beginning and a deep sense of poignancy in the conclusion:

> And your toes, passengers of the extreme
> clustered on your dough-white body,
> say how they miss his feet, the thin elegance of his ankles.
> (S-HC 25)

Often poignant, as in the lovely, haunting "*Liebeslied,*" some of the poems are as lyrical as any in *In an Iridescent Time.* In "Names," the internal rhymes offer the reader as rich an inheritance as all the "plants on the mountain" with their names like "pennyroyal, boneset, / bedstraw, toadflax—from whom [the poet tells us] I did descend in perpetuity" (23). Through the poem, repeated sounds of "tree," "fertility," "to me," and "perpetuity" emphasize the strength of this naming, the continuity of the inheritance from the mother's family. The music in this volume is far more intricate than that of previous collections; a study of sound in Stone's poetry deserves a volume unto itself.

This is a book that, like the poet's mama in "Pokeberries" (as Donald Hall has observed), splits language in two. The next-to-last poem in the section of new poems in *Second-Hand Coat,* "Translations," may well be the book's tour de force. Here we find one of the collection's most powerful characteristics, a tone of understanding and forgiveness and even, through anger and aversion, as Sandra M. Gilbert observes, a deep, forgiving love.

And laughter. "Women Laughing," for instance, is a poem of this collection that incorporates all the shimmering lyricism of *In an Iridescent Time* with a new complexity, a richer, maturer vision:

Laughter from women gathers like reeds in the river.
A silence of light below their rhythm glazes the water.
They are on a rim of silence looking into the river.
Their laughter traces the water as kingfishers dipping
circles within circles set the reeds clicking;
and an upward rush of herons lifts out of the nests of
     laughter,
their long stick-legs dangling, herons, rising out of the river.

(S-HC 52)

Ruth Stone's poems are indeed "nests of laughter," from which rise not only enormous humor but wide flights of wisdom. With *Second-Hand Coat*, Stone's poetry has risen to the stature of the finest poetry being written today.

Note

1. All quotations of Ruth Stone's speech come from my 5 August 1989 interview with her.

Works Cited

Blake, Patricia. "A Room of Their Own." *Time* 22 December 1980: 84–85.

Fay, Julie. "Art in Obscurity." *The Women's Review of Books* 6.10–11 (1989): 18.

Gilbert, Sandra M., Wendy Barker, Dorothy Gilbert, Diana O'Hehir, Josephine Miles, Tillie Olsen, Charlotte Painter, and Susan Gubar. "On Ruth Stone." *Extended Outlooks: The Iowa Review Collection of Contemporary Women Writers*. Ed. Jane Cooper, Gwen Head, Adalaide Morris, and Marcia Southwick. New York: Collier, 1982. 323–30.

Hall, Donald. "Entire Histories." *Hungry Mind Review* (Spring 1988): 3.

Mayes, Frances. Rev. of *Second-Hand Coat*, by Ruth Stone. *San Jose Mercury News* 10 July 1988: 24.

6 *The Poetry of Ruth Stone*
Norman Friedman

No beginner at age forty-four when she published her first book, *In an Iridescent Time* (1959), Stone had mastered the elegant formal conventions of that era, learning her craft from the likes of John Crowe Ransom, Dylan Thomas, Wallace Stevens, Richard Wilbur, and Theodore Roethke, along with nods in the direction of the Elizabethans and Cavaliers, Browning, and Robinson. In other words, as with many other women poets of the fifties—Sylvia Plath and Adrienne Rich, for example—she learned her craft by attempting to express a female vision through a male medium.

Nevertheless, within the largely regular forms of these early poems is heard a complex feminine voice, compounded of the artful naïveté of fable and tale and the deceptive simplicity of a sophisticated artist—who is also a daughter, lover, wife, and mother. That voice is as preternaturally responsive to marriage, family, and human solitude as to animals, landscape, and seasons. Given to gorgeous diction, eloquent syntax, and powerful statement, along with occasional colloquialisms, this book contains nothing callow or unformed, although it does appear marked—at least from the perspective of time—by a somewhat studied artfulness. This impression is borne out by her own growth as she develops and explores the varied possibilities of her unique voice.

As it happened, that development was given a tragic impetus that no one could have foreseen. There is a conspicuous silence of eleven years before her next book, *Topography and Other Poems* (1970), appeared, and the cause of that hiatus—as well as of its fruit—may have been related to her poet-scholar husband's unexpected and inexplicable suicide in 1959, when they were in England, leaving Stone and her three daughters to fend for themselves. She returns repeatedly here, and in subsequent volumes, to this devastating experience, and without ever over- or underplaying it, somehow manages to survive it and grow strong, as Hemingway's Frederic Henry says, in the broken places. There is thus a deepening—albeit a painful deepening—of her emotional range, accompanied, as one might expect, by a corresponding roughening of rhythm and diction.

Two other factors were no doubt also operative: the general loosening of poetic structure and style among many of the formal poets, spearheaded by Robert Lowell's reaction to the Beats during the sixties; and the emerging women's liberation movement of that same decade. While Stone never becomes programmatic or political—impulses that she has deliberately and consistently avoided—she was enabled to deal more directly and forcefully with her own experience. If that experience necessarily went deeper, it nevertheless remained pretty much focused on the personal. Stone is a Keatsian poet "of Sensations rather than of Thoughts," although like Keats she is certainly not without thought, so occupied with responding to the pressures of the lived life that she cannot afford the time for philosophizing and moralizing.

Topography, then, deals with her first attempts to come to terms with her husband's death, her responses to people around her, her return with her daughters to the seasons of Vermont, her subsequent travels, and her continuing growth as a poet, parent, and person. She begins using more direct speech and unrhymed free-verse lines of variable length—not, however, without her characteristic touches of elegance.

In "On the Mountain," for example, she waits in the October dark along with a woodcock and the fireflies, watching "the white haze of the universe," and she concludes:

> The summer is in me like a readiness for flight,
> And I search among the signs
> For the flare, polestar, pulley toward the edge.
>
> (*TOP* 44)

In "Birds," after looking at birds in a museum with her daughters, and after they learn how to birdwatch for themselves, she becomes aware of "the vireo or warbler" and "goes to the brush where they are hid; / Trying to answer, here, here, I am here" (56). And in "Changing (For Marcia)" she writes to her eldest daughter, noticing the changes in her, and reflects at the last:

> Love cannot be still;
> Listen. It's folly and wisdom;
> Come and share.
>
> (*TOP* 86)

That she regained her voice and creative will at this time is shown two years later by the publication of her third book *Cheap: New Poems and Ballads* (1972)—each of these last two volumes containing a hundred pages or more of new poems. Here we find her risking relationships with other men while still trying to deal with her husband's death and loss of their life together, and she mines an iron vein of mordant wit to make bearable that bitterness. Some of her lines strike a late-Plathian note of barely contained hysteria:

> I hid sometimes in the closet among my own clothes.
> It was no use. The pain would wake me
> Or like a needle it would stitch its way into my dreams.
>
> (*C* 10)

"I am disguised and travel with strangers," she feels (11). She hears sounds from the adjoining apartment:

> And I think
> Is this the way it will be?
> And I listen
> With my ear against the plaster.
>
> (*C* 26)

But near a barn, young bulls are bellowing: "What they are saying is out of their separateness. / This is the way it is. This is the way it is" (46). Thus is found some kind of solace in the germinative vitality of nature, repeated in "Cocks and Mares," which concludes with a marvelous evocation of female power:

> . . . the wild mares
> Come up out of the night fields
> Whistling through their nostrils
> In their rhythmic pounding,
> In the sound of their deep breathing.
>
> (*C* 54)

She is "still at the same subject," she announces in "Something Deeper,"

> Shredding facts—
> . . . .
> After something deeper
> That did not occur
> In all the time of making
> And preparing.
>
> (*C* 96)

Second-Hand Coat: Poems New and Selected came out in 1987, after a fifteen-year gap—nevertheless a very productive time— and contains forty-six new poems. Along with exploring her evolving feelings about her lost husband, she probes more deeply into her childhood years and early family memories. Once again she balances between "fertility/futility" ("Pine Cones") and in addition reaches a new level of outrageous fantasy, as in "The Latest Hotel Guest Walks over Particles That Revolve in Seven Other Dimensions Controlling Latticed Space," and satire, as in "Some Things You'll Need to Know Before You Join the Union." In the former, in which there is a rare mention of recent public events, a woman in an old hotel room confronts a strange android in the closet, while in the latter, a "poetry factory" is described where

> The antiwar and human rights poems
> are processed in the white room.
> Everyone in there wears sterile gauze.
>
> (*S-HC* 49)

The Solution, a chapbook of eighteen poems, was published two years later and adds yet another new note: the emergence of Stone's other self, her doppelgänger, as in "The Rotten Sample," "The

Woman in the TV," and "The Ungrateful." And "Bird in the Gil-
berts' Tree" is truly remarkable, beginning with the question, "What
is that bird saying?" and continuing on to give in verbal form what
is strictly nonverbal, a tour de force worthy of Lewis Carroll: "And
you, my consort," says the bird to its mate,

> my basket,
> my broody decibels,
> my lover in the lesser scales;
> this is our tree, our vista,
> our bagworms.
>
> (*Sol* 7)

Who Is the Widow's Muse?, which came out in 1991, makes of the
doppelgänger a dramatic and structural device, in a sequence of
fifty-two relatively short lyrics (perhaps for a year's cycle), plus a
prefatory poem as introduction. Here the muse, a realistic—not to
say caustic—voice, serves to limit and control the operatic tendency
of the widow's voice in her endless quest for ways to come to terms
with her husband's death. As a result, the tone is a miraculous blend
of desolation and laughter, a unique achievement. And at the end,
when the widow still wants to write "one more" poem about her
loss, the muse "shakes her head" and, in an almost unbearably
compassionate gesture, "took the widow in her arms" and concludes: "'Now say it with me,' the muse said. / 'Once and for all
. . . he is forever dead'" (*WM* 59). Thus is Stone solving, in her
own particular way, the problem of expressing a female vision
through a female idiom.

Simplicity (1995) contains all of the poems that originally appeared
in *The Solution*, plus close to a hundred additional pages of new
work. Although there are six or eight poems dealing with her lost
husband, they are more in the way of memories of their early
years than lamentations for his death—some are almost unbearably
tender—and the remainder of the volume is brimming with variety
and vitality. This variety and vitality are of a peculiarly dark cast,
however, for Stone has emerged from her struggle at the age of 80
with a profound sense of the scars that sorrow can leave upon us.
But her sweep is also broad, and her focus can shift from grimy

particulars to the cosmic void in a line or two, from a minute sight of the ordinary to the surrealistic vision of a nightmare.

Through a train or bus window, she takes in the seasons, weather, and cornfields of the Midwest; she notes the loneliness of her fellow passengers seeking solace in casual contact; and, looking past filling stations on two-lane blacktops, she muses on the small town variety stores and trailer parks, the supermarkets and shopping plazas. She has mastered the poetry of passion, sex, and death; of the apocalypse awaiting us amidst the ordinary; and of the stubborn, irrational will to live in the face of our certain extinction.

"The Artist" is exemplary, portraying the artist in is own painting—an oriental scroll "four hundred years old"—ascending a mountain toward a temple above. Although he's been traveling all day,

> . . . You see
> that he can't make it before dark. . . .
> And yet there is no way to stop him. He is
> still going up and he is still only half way.

> (*Sim* 96)

Work Cited

Keats, John. Letter to Bailey. 22 Nov. 1817.

7 An Interview with Ruth Stone: 1973
Sandra M. Gilbert

I first met Ruth Stone at Indiana University in 1973. We were both teaching creative writing classes and courses in modern poetry. But I had a regular tenure-track position while Ruth was on a visitorship, one of a series of temporary jobs that kept her busing around the country from one campus to another for more than twenty years.

Ruth's ordeal-by-Greyhound (she refuses to fly but once threatened to produce a collection entitled "Desperate Buses") came to a happy end when the creative writing program at the State University of New York at Binghamton was perceptive enough to offer her a permanent position in 1990, thereby making her one of the few academics who first achieved a tenured professorship at the age of seventy-five. But at that time in 1973, when I had just come to know her (and decided to do this interview), it seemed as though she had started teaching too late to establish herself in comfort at any one school. That fall at Indiana she was already in her late fifties, and most department chairmen evidently thought of her as a bad business deal, too near retirement to be worth an investment of tenure and all its attendant "perks."

Besides, I feared that Ruth was too vivid, too shabby, too frank, too mysterious, too much a *real poet* and thus too *strange* for tenure. Although students flocked enthusiastically to her classes (and still do), I worried that she alarmed her colleagues and unnerved administrators. Looking sibylline, she would tell deans her visions of their secret wishes—and she would be right. Plainly, therefore, she was "wrong" for academia. Because of this "wrongness," indeed, when I did this interview she seemed to me to have become, besides a woman I love and a poet I passionately admire, a paradigm of what I once called a "lost" woman writer.

Ruth had always been a vivid and brilliant poet, as all the essayists included in this volume testify, but the lucidly articulated pain, the grievous clarity, and the bitter music that now mark her work and that were, for me, associated with both her losses and her "lostness," were born in 1959, when her husband died and she was left with three young children, no job, little money. At first, she tried to raise her family in the old farmhouse on a Vermont mountain that was her only remaining asset, but the winters were deadly, and besides, she needed a salary, so there followed the exhausting round of visitorships in which she was trapped when I first encountered her.

Even as she spun around the country on "desperate buses," however, Ruth preserved both her aesthetic integrity and the terrible clarity of her vision, and she preserved them with the élan, even insouciance, that seems to me to characterize her responses throughout this interview from the early seventies.

Our conversation was taped in April 1974 at my kitchen table in Bloomington, during several meetings. After it was transcribed, I edited it (lightly) into its present form.

Gilbert: When did you begin writing?

Stone: I began writing when I was approximately six and a half or seven years old, and when it happened I did it and then I forgot I did it. I did it and then I found the poem afterwards. And the next time I noticed it.

Gilbert: Why do you suppose you did it?

Stone: Oh, I don't know. I think that it was just my subconscious working. My mother read poetry—Tennyson—to me from the time, apparently, she started suckling me at her breasts. She loved Tennyson deeply. *The Idylls of the King* and all that. And she read them aloud to herself as she was nursing me. She had this big leather bound book of Tennyson. And it probably had a deep influence on me. Then all through my infancy and my young life and even into my adult life my father played drums and all kinds of percussion instruments. He was an intense musician. He never ceased being that. Music was a main love of his life.

Gilbert: Did he work at it? Was that his job, or . . .

Stone: Oh yes, but his father made him learn the printing trade, because his father was in total despair over this boy being a musician. He had no faith in it at all. My grandfather was for many years a member of the legislature in Indiana. He was one of those who wrote the first child labor laws for the state. A wonderful man but nothing remotely related to a musician. His wife was a writer and a painter, though. As well as raising seven children she kept her easel up in her kitchen. Painted hundreds of pictures, wrote several novels, wrote wonderful poetry, was a great wit. I adored my grandmother. And my great-aunts wrote poetry too, and they were musical and painted and all that sort of thing. My uncle Rodney is a gifted writer. He still writes and is nearing seventy. My daughters also write—Marcia writes fine poetry and prose, and Phoebe has written a novel, and Blue Jay [Abigail] two novels. Also, Phoebe is an amazing artist. My mother painted and my sister Elsie paints wonderfully well, and writes too.

Gilbert: So all the poetry was in the blood.

Stone: It was, it was indeed, although I was really unaware of it until I was in my twenties and long after I had started writing. The first poem, certainly, I wrote without knowing I'd done it—and I found that poems came with this mysterious feeling, and it was a kind of a peculiar ecstasy. I can't describe it. I would feel the thing coming and it would rush . . .

Gilbert: A physical feeling?

Stone: A physical rush coming through. And then the poem would write itself. And I would write it from the inside out, upside down, bottom up, everything. I mean, the thing knew itself already. I didn't know it. *I* didn't know it, it just appeared, it would just all come out. And I can remember running into the house, blindly groping for pencil and paper.

Gilbert: Did your mother write them down for you?

Stone: No, she didn't write them down for me. My mother kept this amazing distance from me about all this, but she loved it. And I didn't know she loved poetry, even. I didn't have any memory that she'd read poetry to me.

Gilbert: It's an interesting question: where does a child who's seven years old get the idea of writing a poem?

Stone: I don't know, but I know my daughter Blue Jay used to say them and I'd write them down when she was in the bathtub the way your mother did for you. This is the thing that has made me feel all children are poets and the parent who loves the poetry is the one who preserves the poet. It's the parent who isn't perceptive who kills it. Otherwise, we'd all be singing birds.

Gilbert: Do you feel children's poetry is an attention-getting device, though? Someone once suggested that to me.

Stone: No, I didn't need to get attention. I was the oldest child. And my mother concentrated a great deal of attention on me when I was little. My father used to read to me, too. We'd go and meet him down at the streetcar line. And he'd be carrying his box of candy—really good candy—and a new record. We had a wind-up Victrola and my father would bring home classical music and we'd listen to music and then he'd read to us. And of course it was just enchantment.

Gilbert: I'm interested in the fact that he was a drummer.

Stone: He was not only a drummer, he was a gambler, he was loving, he was weak, he was—

Gilbert: You're defining the poet. All poets are drummers, gamblers, and printers.

Stone: Printers and weak.

Gilbert: Weak and strong.

Stone: Weak and strong. And when he died, an amazing thing happened. It seemed as though thousands of people crept out of the cracks all over Indiana. He had friends all over the country that just adored him. Friends that we didn't know anything about.

Gilbert: You grew up in Indianapolis?

Stone: That's right. I went to Shortridge High School, and you know something funny about me? I don't know whether I have a good mind or not, because I was never a student. I learned to read when I was three and I read madly from the time I was three on.

Madly. Read, read, read, read. Seven, eight books a week. All through my childhood. I couldn't keep my mind off print, my eyes away from it. And yet in school I was bored!

Gilbert: What were you reading?

Stone: Everything. Everything. Long before college-age I had read the bulk of English literature. And Russian literature in translation. I mean—do you know anyone who has read when they were a child all of Mark Twain? And you know, my children tease me about Trollope. They say, "Oh yes, mother read all of Trollope by the time she was three." But the truth is that I've read more of Trollope than almost anyone I know.

Gilbert: Did you read a lot of poetry, too?

Stone: No, that I wouldn't read. I didn't read poetry. You know why? Almost—oh—from the age of seven on I was so afraid that I would copy someone that I would not read poetry. And I only read prose. Consequently, I am a consummate kind of mind about prose, whereas about poetry I've learned only in the last, say, eight or nine years. Now, I don't know if this is good or bad, but I remember sitting at my little rolltop desk and knowing that all I wanted was to write better poetry. I can feel this reaching feeling that I had then, and really that is, I would say, the blueprint of something in me that never altered. And it never occurred to me to connect it with publishing or with the outside world. It was just me and the poetry.

Gilbert: Yes, but where did that impulse to write better and better poetry come from?

Stone: I just don't know. I don't know. I went through high school without telling people that I wrote poetry, and one woman found out and put a poem of mine in a collection, a yearbook or something, and I was elected to all kinds of honorary things, but I hid the letters. No one knew that I did any of these things. It never occurred to me to want them to know. It was so private. I can understand Emily Dickinson. When I began getting published and when I began knowing about achieving and all that—you won't believe this—it was in my second marriage, with Walter, who was a brilliant man and normally ambitious both for himself and for me. And through him I learned about ambition and recognition and all of those things. Up till then, whatever recognition came to me just happened. It just bumbled along to me. It was really weird.

Gilbert: When did you begin publishing poetry?

Stone: When I was in grade school, someone got me to submit some poems to a city contest. And I won—the whole city thing. And that shook me up because the principal called me into her office and I remember shaking physically over it and not being able to cope with the praise.

Gilbert: When you were in high school did you work on the school magazine?

Stone: Yes, but I didn't know exactly what they were doing. I was always in a fog. I just don't know about my brain. It seems as though I'm always facing something that I don't understand. I seem to have to take things in through my pores somehow.

Gilbert: That reminds me of the poem of yours beginning: "I said to myself, do you have a plan? / And the answer was always, no, I have no plan" (*S-HC* 99).

Stone: No plan, that's the way it's always been, all my life. No, I have no plan.

Gilbert: That special quality of everything being conducted in a fog . . .

Stone: And also, something else: when very hard things happened—like my first marriage was extremely unhappy and very unfortunate—I used to wake up every day and have *forgotten* all the terrible traumas of the day before, of living with a creature who was so alien, who assaulted me in some strange way and I had no defenses. But every day I'd forget all the happenings of the day before and start out again.

Gilbert: And without a plan.

Stone: Without a plan, without any remembrance, without any anger, without anything. Just as though everything was new. The only time all of that deserted me was when Walter died. After Walter died, I couldn't live anywhere except in some sort of dreamlike state in which it seemed as though he had never left me. And also the past kept intervening, you know, and then it was as though there was no present, but only the past. And that kept going on for a long, long, long period of time.

Gilbert: But that implies no future, so you still had no plan.

Stone: That's right. I was in limbo.

Gilbert: Do you feel as though that whole quality of not having a plan is somehow characteristic of women? Because it's interesting that you said before that it wasn't until you met Walter that you understood what it meant to be ambitious.

Stone: Well, I was only ambitious vicariously, through him. That is, he sent out all the poems, he defined the idea of achievement, the excitement, and so forth. And indeed, when our two books came out after he died—my *In an Iridescent Time* from Harcourt and his *Poets of Today IV* from Scribner's—they meant nothing to me. Absolutely nothing. All the reason for doing them had died with him.

Gilbert: Well, to get things more in order, let's go back to what happened when you got out of high school. You went on to college? Or what?

Stone: No. I got out of high school and I married John. My father was too poor to send me to college. I'd known John since I was fourteen. And he kept pursuing me and pursuing me. I had a train phobia about him—a transference is what it's called. I was afraid he was going to get run over by a train, because I didn't want to marry him and he was pressuring me and everybody seemed to think he was right.

Gilbert: In other words, you were here in Indiana and you had no notion of what you wanted to do, and so . . .

Stone: I was writing all the time, reading all the time, and that's it. I was at home and it was the depression and I had this train thing, in which I was afraid John was going to get run over by a train. I feared it terribly. So that I had to spend all my time watching those damn railroad tracks in terrible anxiety. You see, I didn't allow myself to even think an unkind thing about anyone. I don't know why. I don't know where I got such a notion, but I couldn't think anything mean about anyone. You see what I was sitting on. Obviously, I feared and hated him. And instead I had to marry him and save him from the railroad tracks. So when he wanted me to marry him, I married him. Well, we stayed in Indiana a few years and then we went over to Illinois for him to work on his

Ph.D. in physics. And then I went to school, too. And when I went to school, there I met Walter.

Gilbert: By this time you were in your early twenties?

Stone: Yes, and the amazing thing was that in almost nothing flat I discovered who it was I was born to marry, who it was I was born to love. Who was my mate. It was horrible. Here I'd met my mate and I was married to someone else. And my whole marriage was so—I tried to love my first husband the way I loved my family, and I was submissive to him, but he was very domineering, and what I did was start sneaking around, sliding around, hiding from him, and so forth, and finally after a period of several years, my father helped me get a divorce and I married Walter. But by that time Walter was in the Navy.

Gilbert: And you were writing all this time?

Stone: Yes. Oh, at one point I wrote silly things, goofy things. I mean about John. I remember a little doggerel I wrote: "I defend the glacial sweetness of your smile," and it ends up "but I abhor to death your kiss." Just a piece of super doggerel.

Gilbert: But then there was Walter.

Stone: I was really very, very slow growing up, as you can see. Not at all mature. A total baby.

Gilbert: But a lot of people go through that . . .

Stone: I don't think I really started growing up till I was about thirty. Maybe not till I was fifty. I remained so childish.

Gilbert: The idea of not knowing what you're doing seems somehow thematic: "I said to myself, do you have a plan? / And the answer was always, no, I have no plan."

Stone: Well, I really believe society kept me an infant, even though part of me was always mature. I realize that now. Oh, realized it even then. I remember rebelling against all kinds of things, but then I also accepted the idea that men were always more intelligent than I. So that even when I was teaching in Wisconsin I'd defer to male students in my class. It never occurred to me that they weren't more intelligent than I.

Gilbert: That's a very familiar experience for many women, I guess.

Stone: Well, I think women and blacks and—it's just cultural, simply cultural. And it wasn't until a few years ago that I woke up to even doubting any of it, and of course the thing is that since all men were more intelligent than I, I realized that what I had to have in a man was what Walter had, and that was *genius*.

Gilbert: In other words, you felt what you recognized in Walter was that here was somebody who could direct you?

Stone: No, absolutely not. Not only did Walter never direct me, but I never looked to him for any kind of criticism. A part of me has been totally isolated and independent all my life, and that's my writing. And I've never depended on anyone about that—nor ever taken a course or ever asked anyone. But what I adored about Walter was everything else and his own abilities and everything he knew.

Gilbert: But of course he was also a writer, so there was—

Stone: He was a writer, but the truth is, you know, that I felt superior to him. That's just horrible, isn't it? I mean, inside myself, I felt superior. And I couldn't keep from feeling that. Not a kind of aggressive superiority, or even a mean superiority, but a knowing. I have this hideous knowing, especially about prose. And his prose wasn't that perfect, by any means. And so we'd go over his prose and he depended on me. He learned enormously from me, and indeed he did say so.

Gilbert: So you didn't show him poems and—

Stone: Yes. When I was a child I would read my poems to my mother; later I'd read poems to Walter. However, he never said one word except that he loved them. That's all. He was just like my mother. Supportive, and that's all. Whereas with his writing I would say, "This word is wrong, you're repeating here," little technical stuff. That was all. Nothing basic.

Gilbert: So when you met Walter you were writing poetry very seriously.

Stone: Yes, and the reason Walter fell in love with me I'm sure is not only because of our physical attraction to one another but because of the writing.

Gilbert: Had you been publishing things at that point?

Stone: A few things. And when Walter was in the Navy during the war [World War II], he was sending my poems out. But when

I finally got published was when we were at Harvard. Jack Sweeney [director of the Poetry Room at the library] started out to gather the poets, I guess, and somebody told him that I was writing, and then Harvard had me record for them and the *Advocate* published me in about eight different issues.

Gilbert: Walter was a graduate student at Harvard then?

Stone: Yes, after the war, and I just simply went along as his wife. Our daughter Phoebe was born there [in Cambridge]. And then we went to Illinois, where Walter was teaching, and the first thing that happened then, I guess, was that Leslie [Fiedler] decided it was horrible that I wasn't publishing more, so he sent a group of my poems to Karl Shapiro, who immediately took them.

Gilbert: This was when Karl was editing *Poetry*?

Stone: Yes. And as a matter of fact, I got the Bess Hokin award for the poems that year or the next year. And Kirker Quinn wanted to publish my stuff in *Accent*, and I guess Walter sent my poems to *Kenyon* and they took some, and the next thing I got was the Kenyon fellowship. I guess John Crowe Ransom gave it to me because of the poems I had in *Kenyon Review*.

Gilbert: So in other words, the pattern was that you still never had a plan?

Stone: Yes, and not only that, there were always these people who were able to help. Leslie liked my prose. Once he took a story away from me and had somebody type it up. Sent it to *Commentary* and they took it.

Gilbert: How did you feel about all this?

Stone: I was just sort of bowled over by it. It was fun when it happened, it was exciting, but I don't know, I forgot about it.

Gilbert: You were busy with your family?

Stone: You know the funny thing is that—well, maybe because of my father playing drums so much—I really am able to shut out noise. And I would write while I was cooking, I would write while I was doing anything, because I could divide my mind up. You must do it too, because you know you have to when you have kids.

Gilbert: I know. I guess most men can't do that.

Stone: Because they aren't trained to. The funniest time was when I was writing that story that was printed in *Commentary*. I had my foot, I remember, on the door of the bedroom because I'd decided I just simply had to write this story. I wanted to get it down. I put my foot on the door and the children were on the other side beating on the door. And I wrote that whole story with my foot on the door.

Gilbert: So all this time Walter was teaching and you were being a faculty wife—and writing.

Stone: Yes, a faculty wife. Except I'll have to say that Vassar College, even though I was a faculty wife, must have been giving me a little different treatment than usual. I think they were a little bit pleased with me, and eventually they asked me to read my poetry there. I remember they gave me a fifty dollar honorarium to read at Vassar while Walter was teaching there. And while I was at Vassar I was invited down to New York to read at the YMCA. And it was there that I had three publishers approach me. Asked me if they could be my publishers. Those were days when poetry, I guess, meant something.

Gilbert: But all this time it was mainly Walter who was sending things out for you?

Stone: Yes, right. He was a fabulous typist and a fabulous everything.

Gilbert: When you think about it now—

Stone: Why did he do it?

Gilbert: No, why didn't you do it?

Stone: I don't know. Why don't I do it now? I never do it. I don't know. It's so much trouble. I guess I really forget. Honest to God, I forget. I have poems mixed in with bills, letters, junk, and when I was really sick a few years ago I thought, why don't I do what Walter used to do? He was starting to organize everything.

Gilbert: But you know, I'm sure this will sound as though you're entirely planless—yet I don't really believe it. I really believe that there's a part of you that's very cold and keen about your poetry. Very purposeful and disciplined.

Stone: I'll tell you something. About the writing itself I care enormously, and I think the difference between the person who is a writer or who becomes an artist and the one who does not become an artist is the obsession. And there's no question in my mind but that I'm an obsessed person—about the art. I'm obsessed. It's obviously—except for my emotional commitment—the most important thing in the world to me, and I can't believe that it isn't important to other people and I'm always amazed when it isn't.

Gilbert: And your sense of form in poetry is very keen, very disciplined. The sense of form in *In an Iridescent Time*—where does that come from, do you think?

Stone: People are always talking about my sense of form. Well, I think it's just built into me.

Gilbert: You master very complicated forms.

Stone: But I thought I was just making them up. I used to invent all this stuff, and then later on I discovered that it existed. Of course, it must have been built into my ear very early, by Mother reading poetry. And anyway, the English language simply falls into numerous kinds of patterns, and I think that just because the language is what it is you can't avoid discovering them as you're fooling around. I used to play endless games with poetry, when I was young. And when I won that citywide contest in sixth grade they gave me a book which had all the poetry forms. And I used to write sestinas and all the French forms. I would just have loads of fun playing with all these patterns.

Gilbert: Do you revise poetry a lot?

Stone: Yes, enormously. I used to be under the impression that I wrote everything in fifteen minutes. But the truth is that I used to work eight hours at a time and not even know it. It would seem like fifteen minutes, but it would start with dawn and would end at dark. I concentrated very hard and I sometimes wrote as many as twenty sheets on a single poem, but I would have thought that I'd written it right down, bing, bing, bing, and why I thought that I'll never know. I worked very hard. And sometimes it took me a year or so to write a poem, and some poems I wrote in a day and sometimes I'd write three poems a day.

Gilbert: One of the poems I love best in *Topography* is the one called "Metamorphosis"—

Stone: Now I can remember sitting down in my living room at the farmhouse and writing that poem, and it just came out like that. Sometimes it just comes out like that. I would say maybe half the poems in that book were written like that. The other half would take page after page after page.

Gilbert: Perhaps the reason "Metamorphosis" came so easily is because it had so much to do with what was happening in your own life, in that time after Walter's death? I feel as though there was a big change in you, in your poetry, as a result of that—

Stone: Yes, well, definitely, definitely. Sometime in that year after he died I remember saying aloud or saying to myself, "The bird has died." It's exactly what happened. I really felt that the bird in me had died.

Gilbert: This was after you came back from England?

Stone: Yes, we went to England—it was so wonderful to go— he had this sabbatical, he had the American Philosophic money, and he'd just sold a story to the *New Yorker* and he'd had an article printed in *Partisan Review*—

Gilbert: And you had a book coming out.

Stone: I had had my book accepted, and he had had a book of poetry accepted by Scribner's, and Doubleday had given him an advance on a novel—

Gilbert: And so you went to England and you were living in Cambridge?

Stone: Yes, and just having an unbelievably good time, kind of mysterious, like swimming in a strange undersea world. And then he died. And then—nothing seemed very real. Nothing seemed very real for a long time. Fifteen years, sixteen years, we lay—we lay every night of our lives together, wrapped in each other's arms. We really loved each other. We were really—he thought we were twins. And you know, the funniest thing is that I used to have dreams about this dusky lion that was sort of playful and I was rather scared of him, but I liked him and he would bounce around the outside of my house, and I didn't realize till after Walter was dead that he was a Leo. And he used to say we were twins. He felt we were twins. And I'm a Gemini. And you know, we weren't conscious of astrology at all.

Gilbert: What did you do then? After he died?

Stone: I went home. With the children. And then I went to work for Wesleyan University and then I just slowly lost my ability for remembering. I couldn't remember anything. I just forgot more and more and more things. I couldn't sleep; I didn't sleep for a year except in little snatches. And you know, it has taken me—how long has it been?—it's taken me a long time to become . . . They say people get over sorrows or shocks but—

Gilbert: Not something like that.

Stone: I think that now, you see, now, I don't suffer the way I did.

Gilbert: But you still suffer. I can feel that.

Stone: You know, the pain came in waves at first, it came in waves so fast.

Gilbert: But then lots of things happened to you after that. I mean, painful as it was, still I think you changed in an extraordinary way, a good way.

Stone: Well, I had to. I had to become competent in a lot of things that I hadn't done. I had to continue taking care of the children, running the house. I began gardening, making fires, cutting wood, hauling oil.

Gilbert: And it seems to me there was a great change in your poetry. The first book is by a young woman sitting in the sun, and being very witty and talented, and the second book is by somebody who's been told even though she wanted to stay in the sun to go into the shade. And she goes into the shade to the cold. It's somebody who's not shivering, she's just sitting there cold but she's not going to say that it's cold.

Stone: Life altered me. Experience altered me. Suffering altered me. Having to endure and be strong altered me. Having not to—not being able to—cry altered me. I didn't cry, but I didn't talk for a year, either. I couldn't talk. I couldn't even stand up straight. I've been told I couldn't stand up straight, I shuffled. Shuffled, and then that line "I shuffled and snuffled and whined for you" (*S-HC* 62).

Gilbert: But then your recent poems are much more amused, ironic. The writer isn't in the sun or in the shade. I don't know where she is. Singing in the rain?

Stone: I don't know either, I really don't. It's funny all those bawdy poems that I wrote two or three years ago.

Gilbert: That's why I keep getting back to "Metamorphosis." It's this sort of Yeatsian metamorphosis from one stage to another.

Stone: Actually, I think that's what happens to you anyway.

Gilbert: Later on after Walter's death you began teaching, didn't you?

Stone: Yes, first at Radcliffe, then at Wellesley and Brandeis and Wisconsin and Illinois, and so forth.

Gilbert: Do you feel teaching has changed you? Do you feel it influences your poetry?

Stone: No, no. But I find that it's a lot of fun to do for other people what I think my mother did for me, and that is, you know, to give them some kind of support. And also it's fun to recognize and to come across their originality, their mind, their points of view. It's fun. And it's fun to help them where they need help.

Gilbert: With their art, right? But not with the "game" of poetry? I mean the game of making it.

Stone: Oh, that game.

Gilbert: The whole game that people play—and what's characteristic of your career as a poet is that you haven't played it and—

Stone: I haven't, but you know I think it's great when poets are well known. I love it when poets get attention.

Gilbert: But at the same time you don't strive for it, you don't—

Stone: Well, I don't know how. I don't know how to go about it. I think I'm handicapped by being a woman, and I have no question but what had Walter lived we would have somehow been different. But you know, if you're playing power games and if you're fascinated by that sort of thing, it takes up all of your mind. It takes up all of your imagination. You can't do that and be something else. I can't. Let's see if there have been times in my life when I've been absorbed by something. Yes, my land, the farm I have in Vermont. And I find that it can take over—chopping wood, building a cold frame, you know, it just takes over. I find that where I'm at ease best—and life isn't worth it if you aren't at ease with yourself—is when I don't think too much or too highly of any of these things, but when I respect, just respect, the good things that happen.

8　An Interview with Ruth Stone: 1990

Robert Bradley

Bradley: You remarked that we write our own poems because we need to write them, but we love other people's poems in a different way.

Stone: You know, the illuminations of others hit you much more strongly. As a matter of fact, you're swept away by them because you didn't make them; you didn't have them. We constantly thirst, we live to suck in everything.

So the work of others is beautiful. It's a great gift. Maybe the work has more meaning for us, and certainly we are able to enjoy the great pleasure of it—knowing the work of another's mind. You not only know that we are not alone in our feelings, but you learn previously unconsidered ramifications of those feelings. Empathy. Sadness for the other. Joy for the other, which enlarges us, so that we are not this isolated sack of blood and so forth walking around; so that, in some way or other, we experience how the fluid that we all live in connects us.

When we're doing our own writing, of course, we're taking it out of our own reservoirs. It comes from what's already entered in, and we bring it out. We need to. It's very important to bring it out of ourselves.

Bradley: Why do you think that is so?

Stone: Because it's in the dark in there. Your mind, as it works, is constantly reviewing things. Language goes on electrically, or whatever it does in there; it's a dark process, a kind of auxiliary involuntary nervous system. When you write, bring out language and experience, you're bringing out consolidated moments. In a way, they represent a great span of time even when they're only referring to a single moment; they're the condensation of a great deal of time and have accumulated all of the overtones and significance of other dramas and added meanings. We bring it out and momentarily we are amused and amazed at the new complexity that occurs, at the significance and the . . .

Bradley: Achievement?

Stone: Well, I don't know if it's achievement; you present a new connection when an incident or experience is made into language. It acquires a deeper significance. As we act, moment by moment, we're spontaneous and right at the edge of time—"right now." Although it feels substantial and real, present experience is thin compared to when you speak of it later, after it goes into the mind and comes out again with all of its connections to memory, to the rhythms of the body, and to the history of language and the rhythms of speech. Once an experience is remembered and written, it becomes much more complex.

When we talk about living in the moment, the moment is just this moment when your mouth is opening, or when you're sitting on this couch. But you live totally in your past. What is this living in the present? It seems like your past drags behind you like a great huge snake or a worm, and there it is. And you do live in it. You can't help but live in your past.

Bradley: Couldn't that snake be more like "trailing clouds of glory"?

Stone: [Laughter] I say trailing coils of snakes behind you. If you consider that moment by moment, as we're going through time, we're moving forward, and then you look linearly backward, it is like you have been making a tunnel, a tunnel through time with yourself.

And you're always at the front here, right at the front, which is this moment now, but, of course, your total self is the totality of what you have lived. We can't just live in the present, or we would be mindless. We live with the past.

Bradley: Well, it's a contradiction, I guess. Even though I'm very much obsessed by my "past," I've also been intrigued by religious practices whose meditations are designed to halt the stream of the past and of personal history and focus the individual being in the experience of the moment—the present.

Stone: And there's a great intensity there. An orgasm, for instance, is a very intense thing because it occupies all your mind and your body electrically, so that it focuses you. It's a tremendous focus in the moment. But of course, it doesn't go on all that long.

Bradley: Well, at least we can look forward to more of them. Do you think we write poems about the loss of that focus? Is there something about loss that makes us count so much on language to make poems?

Stone: Oh, I expect loss and the fear of loss are always a part of what makes life hauntingly beautiful. Death is a great enrichment of your consciousness because of the constant possibility of loss, which enhances the exquisiteness of the moment, of what you have.

Bradley: In your poems, I find a similar tension between corporeal loss and pleasure—the drama of how temporary our lives are. In your poem "Nuns on the Bus," the characters seem almost unworldly by virtue of their "habits," so to speak, their clothes. Yet underneath, it's just matter going about its business in "the temporal body, the vessel of love" (*Sim* 22), as you put it in the poem. Have you always been taken by that kind of contradiction between . . .

Stone: Between what? Our concept of what we think of life and what we actually are? Well, I think there is almost no separation. To ourselves, we seem to be within looking out, and the "out" comes in. We bring it in. The exterior world comes in through our eyes, in our ears, and . . . really, we live in a medium, and we are that medium's pulse, its heart. Yet we're separate, and the central thing we have to take care of is this creature. It's our obligation, then.

That's the wonderful thing about other works of art. They help us love the other, and we need to love the other for practical reasons and ultimately, it seems to me, for meaning. We make patterns because that's how we're made. We are patterns. I think we are a universe ourselves, that our brains are universes, that our body is a universe, that we are made up of so many individual things that are living together in a great composite, and we call it "I."

Bradley: And sometimes "I" doesn't like where it is.

Stone: "I" doesn't like it and sometimes "I" takes off and does what "I" wants to. [Laughter] If you are a person with a love for language, your culture and your language are the center of the mystery for you. I mean, it is how you work through the endless mystery. Which, of course, you never can work through.

Bradley: You talked about writing poems for as long as you can remember.

Stone: Yes, I didn't find out for some years that my mother read poetry aloud when she was nursing me, and then taught me all those poems by heart so that by the time I was two I knew many poems. What she built into me was both a cadence of the language and a music of poetry and patterns. Later on, when I was able, I wrote all these patterns of English poetry.

Bradley: How did you figure out what the patterns were?

Stone: They came out of me instinctively because obviously my mother had put them into me, but I didn't remember that. When I started writing I was six and making poems, and from then on they were patterned. And many times I used to think I was inventing things.

Bradley: Ballads?

Stone: Yes. Oh, definitely. In grade school I won a citywide poetry contest, and the prize was a book of modern poetry and I think a book of—it must have been Untermeyer's little book—*First Forms*. I used to just spend days, years of my young life, you know—it was a great game to me to play and write all those kinds of forms, and it was so easy. It was just a total joy all the time. I didn't write down most of them. And then I would feel a poem coming from way off, like a train coming; I would feel it physically; and I would rush to the house to get paper and pencil to write it down; and, as I said before, it would come sometimes like it had already made itself up in my head. Apparently my mind, for some reason or another, was like some sort of machine. It would just make me up poems all the time. Very funny.

Bradley: You've certainly served an unusual apprenticeship in forms, a subject of some controversy these days.

Stone: You know, because my father was a musician and played the drums all the time, I really was taught an awful lot of rhythms just through my ear. I found form fun. It was a fun game and I slowly, slowly achieved control over what was so spontaneous. I figure it remained spontaneous in that the voice comes through you. When you hear the poem coming, it comes through you. It starts speaking to you spontaneously. But there are so many complicated things that go into the creation of a poem. I don't know at what point I became more in control over what was an uncontrollable process.

Bradley: So that was when you began to be able to shape the making of your poems?

Stone: I don't know. What is the natural singing mind? You know, it's just primitive—the primitive mind at work. But, at any rate, the funny thing is that from childhood on, this writerly section of myself, which went parallel to my living life, always was there. And I never thought of it not being there. One time I remember it went away for three months when I was in high school, and I suddenly woke up to the fact that it was gone. I was devastated. And then it came back without my noticing it, and it went on. But, you know, it was just a parallel part of my life. It didn't lap over much into my life or interfere with it. It was as though I lived a double life. And being a Gemini, that's okay; I *am* a double.

Bradley: You've seen some changes in the way that women can approach poetry and what they do with art.

Stone: It seems to me that poetry and the arts have been backed up forever in women—these outrageous restrictions both by nature and by culture—and all of a sudden there's this explosion. It's been a long time coming. And, you know, here again we're talking about a moment at the front and the past, because here at the front are all the new mayflies, male and female, and yet the males are getting really blamed for all the past, you see. See what's happening? Because the past is still here, and there it is coming along—

Bradley: Inheritance.

Stone: The inheritance, and more verbal inventions to pass it on with, along with every kind of distorted history. Then we also have all of our memories and . . . the situation certainly isn't simplifying itself, is it?

Bradley: How might these complexities affect young writers?

Stone: Lord, I can't speak for other poets. You see, I am unable to give up that other side of myself, the creative side that goes parallel with me. It goes. There it is. And yet, this side is my life. As I say, it's my doppelgänger.

I can speak for my own life. I have, of course, struggled along as a widow. Earlier on, though, I didn't know what kind of life I could have made for myself as a single woman.

I got married. And I had children. And, of course, I noticed that I was often at the fringe, at the edge, no matter what the group would be. Always during the time when I was a young faculty wife, there was this primitive separation between the men and women. And also the ponderousness of male opinion and so forth. The women would play bridge, you know, the faculty wives . . . it was silly. It was silly because it wasn't true to life. But everyone pretended it was.

Bradley: Did it irritate you, were you upset that you weren't able to interact more freely?

Stone: Oh no, not a bit. I lived in my own time. I always had this other life of my own. I received a Kenyon Fellowship. People were respectful about what I did. But I think what happened to women then was that they were treated as though they were bright children.

Bradley: You had to watch what you said.

Stone: I was very careful. Men were always "brighter" than women; no woman was as bright and as capable as a man. I thought that, in order for me to be what I wanted to be, I had to be better than anyone in the world, which made me know I had to work very hard.

Bradley: And you did. How did you work?

Stone: I concentrated and took in as much as I could. I started reading when I was three, and I've read in all directions all my life. Women who love to write poetry are the hagfish of the world. We eat everything. We eat the language. We eat experience. We eat other people's poems.

Well, that's the way it was for me. I couldn't let books alone. I read all night. Mother would get up and turn off the light. She'd go back to bed, and I'd turn the light on and read all night and then get up and go to school.

Bradley: And then as an adult, you returned to school again as a teacher. You've taught in a great many universities and have seen the rise of writing programs. What's your feeling about them?

Stone: You know, I think it's wonderful that the universities have taken in creative writing. Of course, since they did, poetry did become more commercial and more businesslike. There's more evaluation and more ambition. But overall it's wonderful because our culture was in danger of forgetting about poetry, and I think universities helped to save it from neglect.

Bradley: You said you felt a deep obligation as a teacher.

Stone: If you're going to assume responsibility for a group of writers—even though you know each makes his or her own work—there is an enormous responsibility. The responsibility is not to thwart the work or its inspiration. That's number one. Number two is to nurture each individually—each writer and each writer's work.

I believe in the individual artist. A teacher must, somehow or another, focus on this person and this person's work. It takes an enormous amount of energy.

You certainly must disconnect yourself from your own work. Never bring your work to their work, never. That's what I believe in, if you're going to take that responsibility. Then, I think, there are wonderful ways in which you can bring in fresh stimulation, fresh adrenaline; and they can bring it, too; you encourage them to and therefore it becomes the whole. The group then can work together. Then the group can act also as an audience to hear the other and so forth. And the writers themselves can ask questions about what they need to know about the responses and what people think and so forth. You know, there are many ways, but the autocratic way, no. Everything, it seems to me, works for the good of art—if you let it.

Bradley: The model of the young writer looking to the older writer is an ancient model based on a mentor-apprentice relationship.

Stone: Well, there's nothing wrong with learning. There is every-thing to be gained by what has been done by others.

You know, I have learned that whether a person is a good or a bad person can often have nothing to do with whether they are a good or bad artist. Isn't that wonderful? I think that's how you can explain why there are some people who have been given teaching jobs because they may be very good writers themselves, who actually just can't bring themselves to be that interested in another person's work. You might say, they probably shouldn't be teaching, but they have the job because they are very good in their art. And so maybe just by being there and by being themselves they have a good effect anyway.

Bradley: Well, to me that's a strange way to teach. It assumes a hypocritical stance. I mean, they take on the role; or, at least, they take the paycheck.

Stone: You're saying they're doing something dishonest, then. Well, I have my own morality about it. Teaching poetry or creative writing embodies what I know and what I need. I learn enormous amounts from students, and I have a chance to focus on my obses-sion, which is writing poetry.

I obviously have had an obsession with writing all my life. When I think that I have done it all my life and that I wouldn't, couldn't consider living without it, then I have to say that's one of the mainstreams—an obsession of that obsession.

Human beings are born with the ability for language and meta-phors and connections and symbols; everything is natural, as well as all visual arts and music and everything else. We were born to be what we call artists, no matter what degree we have.

Bradley: Some of your poems take liberties with traditional forms, like one of your villanelles that has extraordinarily long lines—the poem "As I Remember," from *The Solution*. What gave you the idea to play with forms one finds in textbooks and make them more "elastic," so to speak?

Stone: I think it might have been my liking Gerard Manley Hop-kins and his ideas about stretching the line. Also, I think it was a kind of unwillingness for me to say that form was as restricting as everyone says it was. I do think that form is probably very difficult for many writers who tend to think in prose lines, and who also feel that form forces them to give up a certain way of saying things. They don't feel free. I quite agree that that's legitimate. On the other hand, I seem to have a very strong, rhythmic way of thinking and writing; so for me form isn't a real problem.

Bradley: You mention that you have a rhythmic tendency in your work. A rhythm in language means that a recognizable pattern has been established. If a discernible rhythm is present, you have a pattern; it's not just meter.

Stone: But I think people who do not write in strict form also have rhythmic patterns. Image making, too, is an issue that poets rally around or against. I love images and couldn't write without them. Some purists or minimalists want to throw out even metaphor and so forth. I think when you pare everything down to flat statement, if you're a powerful enough writer, you can distill the essence of the poem—but to me, that's also a way that you can write if you're not so gifted.

Bradley: How so?

Stone: Well, because there are not many restrictions. You do not need to have a leaping metaphorical mind, or even lean in that direction. You do not even need to have a great imagination. You don't need a sensitivity to rhythm and rhetoric. You can simply state baldly and flatly what you see and what happened and so forth. This is why I feel that writers are being pushed to say stronger and stronger things for shock value; shock value is taking the place of the emotional responses to metaphor and rhythm. So that now you have to have the bloody scene, where the guts are cut open and tumbling out.

Bradley: You mentioned the issue of doing away with metaphor.

Stone: Metaphor, like rhythm, is almost a given. I think we naturally have metaphorical minds, and we naturally have patterning minds, but sometimes we seem to be unable to use them.

Bradley: I think metaphor is the only way we understand anything.

Stone: Of course. "This is *like* this"—we see everything as comparison. Light and dark, everything we see, our minds are comparing mechanisms. So many people think in clichés, and I do feel that the tendency in our time is to speak more and more in a shorthand cliché to one another.

Bradley: And a cliché is a dead metaphor.

Stone: Yes, in a way, poetry is in—as we are in—a time of overexposure for everything. And when that happens, language gets tired. People, writers, and readers become tired of this and this, and so forth. And I think poets are pushed more and more toward unusual, grotesque, and awful things.

Bradley: But, isn't that a reflection in a way of the kind of world we live in?

Stone: Of course. Poetry always comes out of its own time. You can't escape seeing that violence is more and more the subject of everything.

Bradley: That makes me think about the "new" narrative poetry and telling a story in very flat language, distrusting lyric pitch. Can you tell me what is your sense of a lyric poem? How would you distinguish between what might be considered a narrative poem and a lyric poem?

Stone: Most poems are narrative, no matter what you say. I don't think you can name a poem that doesn't have drama at its center.

Bradley: That's what's really curious about all this; even a haiku is a narrative poem.

Stone: Yes, that's right, and it has drama at its center.

Bradley: What about the nature of elegy in your poems? You use a very personal history as your springboard; but before the poem is over, you scarcely even identify the object you're addressing. You use the second person pronoun a lot, and the drama is based on autobiography, but these elegies become much more than just autobiographical. How do you move from the personal to the universal—for example in "That Day," from *The Solution*?

Stone: Oh, that one goes clear out of the solar system. Well, that's just the way I am. I connect. Probably because parallel to my literary development was my interest in the natural sciences. When I was a kid, I used to lie on the grass in the summer and look up at the stars. And then I'd read. I'd get books from the library about the stars. I remember when I saw my first photograph of a galaxy. I still can see it in front of my eyes. It was astounding and beautiful. I completely accepted the whole thing. And then a little later on I read *The Theory of the Expanding Universe* [Fred Hoyle] in its original publication [Phi Beta Kappa]; I never lost that hunger, that need to know more and more and more. I accept the universe. I don't fight against it. I know people who won't look at the stars because they don't want to. They are frightened and they don't want to know.

Bradley: Why do you think they would be frightened by that?

Stone: Well, because it's so huge and also it doesn't seem to have any connection with us. But for some reason or another . . . it makes them fear their own death, their own brevity, their own smallness. It's just overwhelming. But you know, for some strange reason, I don't know why, I never saw it as anything except a longing to know more and more and more. And an acceptance of being "among the all" of whatever it is, but I never wanted to be dominant over it. I never thought we were dominant over it.

The first time I knew about death, I was going to grade school in Indianapolis. The children I was walking to school with knew something I didn't know. And they asked me if I would go up and knock on a door—just go ahead and do it. We'll wait for you here.

I knocked and a man opened the door. And he said, "I'm so glad you came. Come in." And he took me to the parlor and there in that parlor was a casket with this little girl laid out in it, absolutely snow white in a snow white dress. And this was her father. And he said, "You're one of her little friends." He was in tears because no one had come to see her.

I didn't know what to say. It was my very first inkling of death. I hadn't seen anything dead—not even an animal—up till then.

And then I went out and those children had run on laughing, you know. What struck me was the feeling of this mysterious thing—of course I was terrified—this dead child. And the father was so pathetic. The mother must have been prostrate upstairs somewhere and the father was all alone there with that little girl. Those children, they had known her—I hadn't—and they giggled and laughed and sent me in. Isn't that strange?

But you see, that was their fear; they were afraid of it, too. Looking deeply into the starry sky, or being afraid of the universe— it might be, in a way, like looking at your first death.

9 *Poet in the Mountains*
Willis Barnstone

Wang Wei, the Chinese Tang dynasty poet (a.d. 701–761), lived in Deep South Mountain. He was China's nature and metaphysical poet who spoke in conversational detail about everyday things, startling us with his recognition and his poignant sentiments about the human drama. In a late poem, "Escaping with the Hermit Zhang Yin," Wang wrote,

> Across the water in my small cottage
> at year's end I take your hand.
> You and I, we are the only ones alive.
>
> (T. Barnstone and W. Barnstone 156)

Ruth Stone, who, when not instructing in one of her many universities, lives on a mountain in Vermont by the Goshen Gap, shares Wang Wei's candor and intimacy. When she speaks in her poetry it is not to a crowd, which never exists, but only to the single reader, and she and the reader are the only ones alive.

For most of her writing life, Ruth Stone has been a secret poet. Her obscurity means that while she has been amply anthologized and widely published in books and periodicals, has given countless readings and, until her recent distinguished position at SUNY at Binghamton, taught for nearly thirty years as a wandering professor at a new college or university almost each year, sometimes two in a year (Ruth Stone may hold a record for teacher vagabondage), she remains a national secret that her multitude of single readers hold as a personal discovery. Stone's relation with us, the readers, is perfectly in harmony with her acuity in going directly to the poetic truth of an event, which she expresses in words that amaze by their intuitive precision, humor, horror, and compassion. It is appropriate that she be secret, because she is also poor. Her real and poetic house is beautiful and pondered by time, waiting for the next repair to give it new mornings, for she gives away her money to those who need it more than she. Her generosity leaves her free of dollars (she spends virtually none on herself); and while her house may be in need of heat, a new roof, a septic tank, and more bookshelves, her unique solitary alliance with art also directs the vision of her poems, which we see in the very titles she has chosen for two of her books, *Cheap* and *Second-Hand Coat*. Ruth Stone's poverties—her early loss of Walter Stone in 1959, her beloved poet-professor, her economic poverty as she has contended alone with supporting herself and three young daughters through their education and early adult lives—have, like all adversity, kept her lean and real and made her wealthy in her profession, which is her poetry. Her finances also made her turn, by necessity, to her second profession, her teaching; her professor-husband's death eventually led her to replace him in the classroom.

Stone is a legendary teacher of poetry like no one on this side of the century, which has led to many ardent converts to poetry. She has given her full spirit to instruction—she sees, offers plain, honest criticism, and converts by her example. No wasted word escapes her sharp attention. In her encounter with young students, she becomes of their age, an age she has never lost in her poems. And the classroom has alerted her to current material and kept her distinctive prosody, always classical, renewed and fresh. But Ruth Stone finds her inspiration everywhere and anywhere. Each event in her life, whether relating to a rooming house, a meadow, or the suicide's rope, has pushed her further into her knowledge, passions, and art. She is a total artist. Through daring and precise wizardry, she transforms macabre losses into miraculous creations.

Stone has enjoyed, lost, and suffered; and joy, loss, and pain imbue her poems with poetic events and her bluntly surprising metaphors. Her eye and ear affirm that humanity's pain and song are everywhere. And love's expression extends even down into the sea, where in "The Talking Fish" we learn that "There is no choice among the voices / Of love. Even a carp sings" (*TOP* 8). "The

Talking Fish" is one of a hundred poems that bring us to the dirt soul of feeling. She talks to her love, who may be here, gone, or dead, as well as to mountains, atolls, and coral reefs, which she questions about their feelings toward her. She asks whether she is among the jellyfish of their griefs, thoroughly confusing nature and person, while playing with time, which is there to change, provoke memory, and conserve the dead. She sees through time to engender people and their ghosts who remain to talk and be with her. Even weeds measure the time of the sea, moving slowly, staining "the soft stagnant belly of the sea."

As in Chinese poetry in general and always in Wang Wei, nature is for Stone a line of observation parallel to personal reflection. Nature and personal events become interchangeable. As in "The Talking Fish," her fish even talk:

> My love's eyes are red as the sargasso
> With lights behind the iris like a cephalopod's.
> The weeds move slowly, November's diatoms
> Stain the soft stagnant belly of the sea.
> Mountains, atolls, coral reefs,
> Do you desire me? Am I among the jellyfish of your griefs?
> I comb my sorrows singing; any doomed sailor can hear
> The rising and falling bell and begin to wish
> For home. There is no choice among the voices
> Of love. Even a carp sings.
>
> (*TOP* 8)

Reading this love poem attentively, we discover that she addresses not only the lover whose eyes are red as the sargasso, illuminated and lost in death's sargasso, but the nature of her perceived imagination: slow weeds, diatoms, the belly of the sea. She asks him, his mountains, and objects of the ocean whether they desire her. Does nature return her desire? Stone places herself also with nature. She is a jellyfish and wants to be included among the significant jellyfish by going through her lover's water world. "Am I among the jellyfish of your griefs?" We cannot be certain, yet we suspect that she has given nature the powers to respond. She does assure us, however, that any doomed sailor longs for return to home. The circle of desires has no choice. And so the voices of communication of desire, song, and sorrow pervade the earth and ocean. "Even a carp sings." There is no thing so high or so low that it doesn't feel and doesn't sing.

Everything enters the scenes of Ruth Stone's poetry: a mountain and eggplant, trash and junky possessions, time, and passion. She is fair in seeing the whole world as a verbal construct, which, as in Kabbalist practice, she translates into her poems of common meditation, feeling, and beauty. Ruth Stone's first volume, *In an Iridescent Time* (1959), contains the essence of her subsequent books. In it she establishes her language and images, which she elaborates with great daring in subsequent volumes. In *Iridescent Time* we find the perfectly chosen word, with no froth or dross; yet at the same time she is never guilty of a crabbed line for the sake of economy. In her early poems she is more formal, which was characteristic of the era, yet never stiff or fashionably ceremonial as, say, were the early W. S. Merwin or Adrienne Rich, who like Stone were to move from formalism to their own special speech. Like James Wright and Theodore Roethke, who also began with altered traditional forms, the poet's voice was only enhanced by the strictures and musical demands of the forms. Although death, as the ghost lover, already appears in this volume, which with all its transformations infuses her later books with such profound feeling and blackly joking humor, there is also a sensual joy of country and body unheard in any other American poet. She does not go to the Song of Songs for her allusions, but she might have, for her lines are passionately rich with pastoral retreats and morning and night love. Take the poem "Orchard." Here she is not the jellyfish, but the mare. In the tradition of love, sexuality, and horses—going back to the Greek lyric poets, to Ibykos's "swift trembling chariot stallion" (Barnstone 114) to Anakreon's "copulating horses" (Barnstone 122) and Sappho's "supreme sight of cavalry on the black earth" (Barnstone 66)—Stone's apple trees, flocks of finches, and dancing mare shake the sexual hills with music and young triumph.

> The mare roamed soft about the slope,
> Her rump was like a dancing girl's.
> Gentle beneath the apple trees
> She pulled the grass and shook the flies.

Her forelocks hung in tawny curls;
She had a woman's limpid eyes,
A woman's patient stare that grieves.
And when she moved among the trees,
The dappled trees, her look was shy,
She hid her nakedness in leaves.
A delicate though weighted dance
She stepped while flocks of finches flew
From tree to tree and shot the leaves
With songs of golden twittering;
How admirable her tender stance.
And then the apple trees were new,
And she was new, and we were new,
And in the barns the stallions stamped
And shook the hills with trumpeting.

(*IT* 33)

The poem is a tetrameter song with lots of rhyme and a driving
physicality reinforced by its limpid regular speech. Its prosody has
the rhythm of dancing women, stamping stallions, and trumpeting
hills. Such joy evokes the sensual Song of Songs woman in new
villages, eating breakfast in unknown fields. It is a woman speaking,
daringly candid as was Praxilla, who more than any Greek poet I
know, in her few extant lines, was able, in a poem about quitting
life, to speak in the most elemental way of what she loved in this
world:

Most beautiful of things I leave is sunlight;
then come glazing stars and the moon's face;
then ripe cucumbers and apples and pears.

(Barnstone 171)

Not concealed, however, in Stone's poem, even amid the splendor
of the sensual meadows, is the "woman's patient stare that grieves."
There is no happiness, of heart or body, without punishment and
grief. Such balance, and the mixing of dream, nightmare, and ordinary scuzzy details from a sordid hotel room or a polluted planet,
keep Ruth Stone's poems off balance and the reader bruised and
astonished. The full grief comes out especially in her later books,
but in the last poem in *Iridescent Time*, "All Noahs," the afflicting
payments of death begin. In this poem about Walter, Ruth has not

yet established her lifelong encounter with her resurrected lover, whom she calls up, accuses of double murder, adores, and lives with in verse all through her poetic life. Here her voice includes only Walter fatally alone, condemned to agony and perpetual dark. The wounded child screams in bed, attempts escape, like Noah, yet not in a pair of living things, but lashed alone in the biblical storm. After agony and exhaustion, he is fated to be the child forever in sleep. The book ends with Walter's tragically deplorable burial (buried at least till the next book):

> No more the child who screaming in his bed
> Fails at the edge of dark to bare his wound
> For binding since none may find the cut;
> Alone, protesting in his head,
> he finds the perpetual dark,
> Though day and night go round,
> And sensing the storm he sets his bony ark
> On a mountain for deliverance against the wind's strut.
> No pairs of living things bear on with him
> In the groaning whirlwind and the gnashing deep.
> He lashes himself alone in his single grim
> And voiceless agony, and as the child, exhausted,
> Finally sleeps, so he may sleep.
>
> *(IT 55)*

As in Dickinson's "I heard a fly buzz when I died" (465), which ends "and then I could not see to see," the repeated verb "see," as Ruth Stone's "sleep," changes meaning in repetition, making death a palpably human, feelable condition. Yet while Dickinson comes to death with failing windows and eyes that won't see, expressing insightful and awful negation, Ruth's man-child comes to sleep by choice, the choice of the suicide, and his decision for fatal peace is all the worse.

Except for two, or possibly three, poems, the material in *In an Iridescent Time* was, as its title suggests, written before Walter's death occured. So Stone's title poem, "In an Iridescent Time," is a poem of radiance before the fall. It is about hanging clothes out to dry. She has not brought a rope into the house of a hanged man—nor removed all possible signs and symbols of the rope, including the poem, after the terrible act has taken place. Inevitably, the rope of the clothesline intensifies a joy captured in the past. The cord is outside, made to hang wash on so it can shine and dry in the sun and provide a center for her young family's union. Her memory of her mother and her mother's sisters becomes a document of transparent pleasure and innocence, ironically drawn, of course, but truly a tub of light from an iridescent time:

> My mother, when young, scrubbed laundry in a tub,
> She and her sisters on an old brick walk
> Under the apple trees, sweet rub-a-dub.
> The bees came round their heads, the wrens made talk.
> Four young ladies each with a rainbow board
> Honed their knuckles, wrung their wrists to red,
> Tossed back their braids and wiped their aprons wet.
> The Jersey calf beyond the back fence roared;
> And all the soft day, swarms about their pet
> Buzzed at his big brown eyes and bullish head.
> Four times they rinsed, they said. Some things they starched,
> Then shook them from the baskets two by two,
> And pinned the fluttering intimacies of life
> Between the lilac bushes and the yew:
> Brown gingham, pink, and skirts of Alice blue.
>
> (*IT* 7)

"In an Iridescent Time" is the most focused and beautiful fifteen-line sonnet I've read. The poem brims with caustic playfulness under her wickedly funny eye. Yet balancing day and night, joy and gloom, sun and death, Ruth will not let us rest. Almost brutally, she places across the page from her poem of ablutions the magnificent "The Magnet," which tells the other side, the dark one. It too has the energy, the breezy, snappy humanity of "In an Iridescent Time," but the light is poignantly transformed. Her fluent, complex, ballad-like rollicking poem talks about her lord, her black-haired lord and young love, who like a fox, a beast, a sheep, a lover, is fatally drawn by an unbearable magnet (inside him or in nature) to his murder in the forest. The poem has a terrible quality, the terror and rumble of bouncing words, which only a Gerard Manley Hopkins or Dylan Thomas or Ruth Stone could concoct. She makes "her coat out of grief." The ending is violent and uncontained as in Greek tragedy:

I heard him coming through brambles, through narrow
   forests, I bid my nights unwind,
I bid my days turn back, I broke my windows,
   I unsealed my locks.

                           (*IT* 6)

In *Topography and Other Poems* (1970), Ruth Stone has gone like
Wang Wei to live in seclusion up on her cold mountain in Vermont,
and there she lives with her "Two-Dollar Chinese Print" (*TOP* 53),
"the white haze of the universe" (44) that pulls her near the edge;
there she also lives with her daughters, one, two, three, whom she
brought up on a widow's purse. She doesn't waste the moment.
There is nothing negative in her life—her lonelinesses, loss, and
longings—that she doesn't recreate into more vivid life, into poems,
into green now:

> In August we carried the old horsehair mattress
> To the back porch
> And slept with our children in a row.
> The wind came up the mountain into the orchard
> Telling me something;
> Saying something urgent.
> I was happy.
> The green apples fell on the sloping roof
> And rattled down.
> The wind was shaking me all night long;
> Shaking me in my sleep
> Like a definition of love,
> Saying, this is the moment,
> Here, now.

                           (*TOP* 37)

If love's apples fell while they were still young and green, no
matter. They rattled down and shook her sleep, defining love. She
will transform them; it is her obsession, duty, and ultimate pleasure.
She will never abandon the now of perception, but also the now
of memory. That's how she will live. Her Vermont house is one
of the main characters in her life, and each room, in addition to
having her fine books—with poems on papers and envelopes safely

stored or lost in them—has rocking chairs, old pumpkin pine bed-steads, a barn-tin roof, delicate blue wallpaper, and windows with rain, orchards, and farmer neighbors directly outside the panes. All figure in the moments of her verse. Close friends come to that house, and after a decade from Walter's death, when she will leave her house, then her student friends come. But in the early sixties, the moment of her Vermont topography is, in reality, no longer enough for her. She needs more, to experience more places, peoples, and events. She is fully separated from the urban, literary, and publishing world. She cannot write indefinitely for storage among her papers. It will take her incredible editor, William Goodman from Harcourt and later from Godine, to seize her poems himself, help type and order them, and bring them out in her first, second, and third volumes. Goodman sent her poems back to the world.

I met Ruth before she went back up to her mountain, while I was at Wesleyan University, where I was teaching. It was less than a year after Walter died. Richard Wilbur had found her a job with Wesleyan University Press. Ruth and I were good friends—we read together—and a year later when she left her job to live winter and summer on the Goshen Gap in the old white-frame farmhouse that she and Walter had bought shortly before they left for Europe, I helped her move her things up north. The next year Ruth found me and my family an old colonial house on a nearby mountain, and so for fifteen years our children grew up, at least in the summers, together. My daughter Aliki published her first book, *The Real Tin Flower* (1968), when she was twelve, in large part because we all shared the poetry rooms of Ruth Stone's ramshackle menage. With Ruth and her daughters, Marcia, Phoebe, and Abigail, along with my brood of painters and poets, it was perfectly natural to write and paint, and we all did so. It was a precious time. Yet the years were passing, and Ruth needed other sources and other places needed her. The isolation and long white winter weren't easy in the other months of the year, and Ruth required a way back from her Edenic May-fresh and solitary harsh–December retreat. I got an idea. One summer in the mid-sixties, on my portable mechanical typewriter, I wrote to over a hundred colleges and universities. I remember, in those pre-computer days, how glossy-thin and ugly the paper was and how broken and painterly the straggling lines, with my typos and erasures, looked on the page. Nevertheless, five good schools quickly responded, offering Ruth a position. So she began another life. She chose to follow the practice of Wang Wei, the Taoist nature poet who spent part of his time as Counselor of Music instructing at the court in Changan (the capital city with a thousand poets) and the rest back at his cottage on Deep South Mountain, where he looked at nature, wrote, and received wanderers.

So Ruth Stone came down from the mountain and saw many new worlds. In summers she drove back up to the Gap. The new pictures from the world below appear in *Cheap* (1972), *Second-Hand Coat: Poems New and Selected* (1987), and *Who Is the Widow's Muse?* (1991). Back among newfound memories (for memories and imagination are her poems' reality) she found a way of making even the most humble and helpless object—a rotting potato, awful, hopelessly condemned to the rot of time, yet, once observed and stilled into ink through her pen—significant. Evil, which is the ticking poison of time, is not to be denied, for it robs vegetable fullness of its form and health, as it stole life from a lover husband. Nevertheless, she will not shy away from time's unmercies. She cuts into the dry earth vegetable and faces its "Dark Conclusions":

> Like cutting the dryrot out of a potato,
> There is nothing left in a moment but the skin
> And a little milky juice. How awful to slice it open
> And find the center fustating, malevolent.
> (A. Barnstone and W. Barnstone 603)

The key ambiguity lies in the words "a moment." The moment is *empty*, because death-time has killed the food's body, yet the potato *fills* the center of the moment with its gruesome, malevolent stink, its bit of milky juice (a memory of better life), and of course it also fills the moment with its dramatic presence, which becomes the poem. So the paradoxes, the antinomies, the deaths and resurrections in all her poems that she confronts (because she cannot bear lies) oblige her to see green ghosts along with fustating potatoes.

As Ruth Stone moves across the down-mountain planet, usually by car, bus, or train (she flies in airspace only in her poems), the landscape explodes with her observations. Her mind is everywhere, in science books, in classrooms, in the ooze of oxygen and in people's toes and shoes, on a railroad platform whose entire histories ravish her. She learns what America is as it puts the butter on its white bread. As with the time-sickened potatoes, she will not kid herself. Even her entire mountain blushes before the reality of death and present sordidness, which, like Baudelaire in his Paris, are always there with dream, hope, and Eden. After the anesthesia of snow melts, she catalogs her people truths and city truths in "Why Kid Yourself":

> Snow, that white anesthesia evaporates.
> It's gone like a lover after the morning paper.
> An entire mountain blushes.
> Everything's been at it.
> Embarrassing bodies are pushing out.
> Plants, animals, swollen with excess
> are straining to keep their balance.
> Two hot days and the population explodes off the circuits,
> jams the sewers.
> Afterbirth reeks in the swamps, gluts the rivers.
> And everything that lived through last year
> is out fattening itself, eating the babies.
>
> (*S-HC* 24)

"It's gone like a lover after the morning paper." Yet despite the newspaper grimnesses, the grotesques of embarrassing bodies, jammed sewers, and all living things fattening and eating babies, it's clear, now and hereafter, the lover is *not* gone. He should reasonably be dead by now, which is why Ruth Stone raises and debates the questions, and which she will do most forcefully in *Who Is the Widow's Muse?* Years earlier, T. S. Eliot wrote, "The readers of the *Boston Evening Transcript* / Sway in the wind like a field of ripe corn." Eliot carries the paper in his hand, walking about as "if the street were time" (16). Thereby he possesses the past. So memory and its truths will not be wiped out by momentary newspaper information. Stone's lover lies in horizontal dry bones down in the dark earth's corrosive years, yet he also lives in the mind's time. She is defeated by an immutable fact in past time and at the same time she conquers time through her mind's pen. The past is real even for a fly. She notes that even a fly, landing on her desk, must think, and not arrogantly,

> where have I been? Where
> am I now? What year is this?

(S-HC 22)

Part of Ruth Stone's impeccable craft of survival, which scans her poems and daytime, is her pleasure in facing the dual facts of grief and laughter, of old photographs and new glimpses, of time's many faces. Imagine how desperately melancholy and fantastically ecstatic to juggle these conflicting physical and spiritual truths, which long to repudiate and mock each other, but which Ruth confronts, her eyes and heart wide open, not letting polemic abolish the rights of the other. The "scar" is one of the body's indelible time-rulers, which we carry for life, and though scars, like the memory they evoke, may fade, they persist, unseen or rediscovered. So the scar is a perfect symbol object for one of her remarkable poems, "Scars," in which she carries on her dialogue with her lover, that is, with a self that includes the constantly evolving and changing person of the ghost. In other poems, she and the ghost recall each other, check each other out, embrace, make love, murder, rescue, compete, and complete. In "Scars," Ruth Stone is hearing him make excuses, child excuses; she acknowledges that he is concealed by her alphabet, and she hears him in the bellowings of animals or chicory flowers. Then she takes off, sees the impossible (which is always her territory), now in a space ship with Argentines; in her final lines the space veterans, like her lost Walter, bring out scars to prove, in one form or another, their existence:

> Sometimes I am on a train
> going to a strange city,
> and you are outside the window
> explaining your suicide,
> nagging me like a sick child.
> I have no unbroken rest.
> Sometimes I cover you
> with an alphabet

or the steers bellow your name
asking the impossible of me.
The chicory flowers speak for you.
They stare at the sky
as though I am invisible.
Often the distance from
here to the pond changes.
Last night a green fire
came down like a space ship,
and I remembered
those people in Argentina
who went inside one
where it burnt the grass,
and forgot their measures
like clabbered milk,
forgot who they meant to be
or suspected they might become,
and later showed the scars
on their foreheads
to everyone,
begging them to believe.

(S-HC 6)

Out in the world, Ruth Stone is walking, riding on buses, or journeying by way of her reading through a shirt factory in Constantinople or the deep iris of the Caspian Sea. The diverse experience, whether immediate, from books or memory, has equal reality before her photographic eyes. She recalls cold borscht in a bare kitchen or is hilarious as in "Curtains" when she combines her familiar ghoulishness with shock:

I want to dig you up and say, look,
it's like the time, remember,
when I ran into our living room naked
to get rid of that fire inspector.

(S-HC 15)

This stanza is followed by the poem's last mock-angry, tragicomic line, which taunts the listening Walter with "See what you miss by being dead?" She is speaking not in the past, but right now, as if to say, Why don't you join in this fun? Why did you kill yourself? Why must I alone dig you up so we can enjoy things together?

In her most recent poems, which appear with increasing regularity in the journals—I wonder if Ruth will soon cease being apocryphal—she brings current novelistic speech to her narrations of days fifty years ago. But she devises a silent, austere woman who knew then what the next fifty years would be, and then she's again looking back, as in "Coffee and Sweet Rolls": "who for years survived on this fiction" (*Sim* 107). So she flips back and forth from one age to another, from one fiction to another, and each is distant, contradictory, and replaceably the same. Her poem ends, however, taking us back, fixed in the past, and while the dark window shade is drawn, it is the perfect ending for a poem that, like good poems, doesn't end. The endless lovemaking is about to start. Already eighty years old, Ruth is of course young and at the height of her powers, which in her case is obvious as it is rare:

When I remember the dingy hotels
where we lay reading Baudelaire,
your long elegant fingers, the nervous ritual
of your cigarette; you, a young poet working
in the steel mills; me, married
to a dull chemical engineer.
Fever of having nothing to lose;
no luggage, a few books, the streetcar.
In the manic shadow of Hitler, the guttural
monotony of war; often just enough money
for the night. Rising together in the clanking
elevators to those rooms where we lay like embryos;
helpless in the desire to be completed;
to be issued out into the terrible world.

All night, sighing and waking, insatiable.
At daylight, counting our change, you would go for coffee.
Then, lying alone, I heard the sirens,
the common death of everything and again
the little girl I didn't know
all in white in a white casket;
the boy I once knew, smashed with his motorcycle
into the pavement, and what was said,
"made a wax figure for his funeral,"
came into me. I had never touched the dead.
Always the lock unclicked and you were back,
our breakfast in a paper sack.

What I waited for was the tremor in your voice.
In those rooms with my eyes half-open,
I memorized for that austere and silent woman
who waited in the future,
who for years survived on this fiction;
so even now I can see you standing thin and naked,
the shy flush of your rising cock pointed toward heaven,
as you pull down the dark window shade.

(*Sim* 106–7)

This recent poem, one of her most powerful, not only doesn't end but excites repeated rereadings. Every line is memorable. All early poems prepare for the next, because she grows ever more common and extraordinary as a poet. I think of the great poets of our century, of César Vallejo in his poor-man's Paris room reading a short story by Daudet between the nipples of his lover; of Rainer Maria Rilke in his exiles wondering who might hear him on earth or among the angelic orders; of Antonio Machado living on "The Street of Abandoned Children," overlooking the grave of Saint John of the Cross, and recalling his young wife, "Leonor," high on graveyard hill in Soria; of Constantine Cavafy remembering, reliving moments of love in his bed over the tavern in Alexandria; of Anna Akhmatova looking at her gray hair in her Leningrad bedroom mirror, seeing her jailed son and executed husband in the glass's multiple images, and smiling like a preferred yellow butterfly as she observes that it is too late for them to kill or silence her. Then, after being the voyeur reader of my companion poets, I think of Ruth Stone's "Coffee and Sweet Rolls" and the woman in the dingy hotel room, lying alone, no luggage, hearing the sirens, waiting for the lock to click and the dark poet to come in with breakfast in a paper sack. These European poets are the American woman poet's kinsmen. Each one, in a unique voice, has written essential poems for our time; they have mixed the personal with geography and the philosophical, and their work is right, memorable, often funny, always passionately moving. We live by their poems, as they did in composing them. In his sonnet "Archaic Torso of Apollo," Rilke said we must change our lives. The poems of Ruth Stone and her kinsmen help us to do so. They help us to survive. I read

Ruth Stone's poetry and feel relieved to be so moved by art, by her art, by all its shapes of candor.

Stone's poetry has resonances from many periods.

In the first lines of the Gospel of John, John forgets that he is a Jew of that intertestamental period, of messiah seekers and apocalyptic visionaries, and he writes like a logical, syllogistic Greek (Greek being then the language of most Jews). He writes the marvelous words "In the beginning was the word," which recall the texts of early Kabbalists (who go further, saying in the beginning was the *letter*) as well as the parallel "In the beginning" lines of Genesis, where God's power resides in the power of the word to create, "Let there be light." A few lines later, John carries his syllogism one step further, saying, "And the word was made flesh, and dwelt among us" (John 1:14).

Stone has lived, created, and survived by the word, and, more, in Johannine fashion, made the word flesh. She knew love, and when it was gone factually, she undid the fact, and resurrected love as flesh through her word. She has resurrected the whole person to haunt, torment, accuse, love, and realize herself. Why should she abandon what once existed in time, but which persists in mind, heart, and her flesh? So (using Henri Bergson's lexicon of *temps* and *durée*) she exchanges public time of the clock, which is socially correct and mechanically measurable, for duration, which is time of the mind and obeys no external rule. By this measure, a lover's death and past time, at least in her mind and word, become fiction and disappear; and her word gives memory a vivid new life, which she passes on to us. Strictly speaking, Stone prefaces John's words "In the beginning was the word" with an earlier segment in the circle of perception. In the Stonean version of creation, in the beginning was the *flesh*, the human body, and only then did the lover's flesh (perceived by the poet) become a word for the poet to utter; she endowed her word with an objective referent, with bodily flesh, accomplished through the poem, thereby making her words signify tangible objects. So while in John we have *word* → *flesh*, in Stone we have *Flesh* → *word* → *flesh*. She accomplished all this by making language into warm things, quite naturally, as good writers do. But in Ruth the process, because of her genius for clarity and simplicity, is fully visible. The circle is complete. Ruth is the maker, and she will throw all things into her pot of creation—time, dream, death, lovers, hatreds, flesh, and words.

In Ecclesiastes, that unusual agnostic scripture about time, love, and vanities, the rabbi preacher tells us that past things are future things, which is what Ruth Stone has told us all her poetic life: "The thing that hath been, it is that which shall be" (1:9). A common man of similar contradictions and diversity, he tells us that time has many seasons under heaven: "A time to weep, and a time to laugh; a time to mourn, and a time to dance" (3:4). Stone has heard the rebel speaker. She sees the vanity of death and goes beyond it, articulating her creed that all things under the sun of the past are hers to bring forward. And she does so, as a secular messiah, raising the dead for herself and us to enjoy. Why not? She needs to. It is fearful, deadly, and cold to cast away the past, especially since it sticks in her mind. She agrees with the speaker in Ecclesiastes who says wisely, "Again, if two lie together, then they have heat: but how can one be warm alone?" (4:11). She has two in her bed of poetry. Sometimes she must wipe some dirt from his eyes and body; usually, they enjoy each other full-blown, with no sign of rot. Stone and the preacher love the meadows and sun and say together, "Truly the light is sweet, and a pleasant thing is for the eyes to behold the sun" (11:7). She willingly gives Ecclesiastes the last word, since it confirms her word of light, it confirms what she says in each poem with all her heart and poetic strength. That last, infinite word is, "The sun also rises" (1:5).

I have connected Ruth Stone with the rabbi in Ecclesiastes, obviously not to show her or his religiosity. The rabbi, who declares himself with the poor and wise, was scarcely a man of any recognizable cloth, and theologians often ask how this wonderful outsider slipped into the canon. The preacher hated dust and death and believed a live dog better than a dead lion. As for Stone and God, no, there is no overt tie. God is not a figure in Stone's poems, unless God is her sphere of time in which she sports around at will—though not without grief. Like Stone, the preacher was a poet and a metaphysician. He said, as she does, "That which hath been is now" (Eccl. 3:15). It sums up Ruth Stone's passionate way of existing. What was is.

In living the resurrection of a passion, Stone follows a universal process of ecstasy. Ecstasy has many presences and voices: existential bewilderment, personal anger, political frenzy, religious bliss, lover's dream, Jorge Luis Borges's otherness, and even Dante's infernal terror. Ecstasy (*ekstasis* in Greek) means to be elsewhere. But one goes to and leaves dream, God, or madness, without a camera. The mystic slips away and returns from the extraordinary to the ordinary, astonished before the loss of the vision. Hence the oblivion. Since oblivion is blurry, the religious or secular mystic lacks the right words to describe the journey elsewhere. Hence the ineffability. Maybe the object of the journey is not there. (Is Yahweh's chariot, Jesus' arms, or the zero of nirvana really there? Probably not). In reality, the nature and translation of the ecstatic experience into a universal symbol depends on how the traveler has programmed and interpreted it. The experience of the uncommon (however it is deciphered) is routine and undeniable. Those who go elsewhere—to be mad, to chat with God, to lie unconscious in dream, or to reside in erotic or spiritual union—are not frauds. We are all ecstatics at one time or another.

Stone knows her lover is in the grave. She's not out of her mind (though she is ecstatic). And she also knows, like the mystics, that what the mind recalls and invents is a significant reality. But the mystic is convinced or deceived that the god-lover is alive and present during ecstasy. For Ruth it is enough to remember. And her experience isn't clouded with oblivion or the ineffable. She is perfectly lucid. After she has resided in the extraordinary, with her artistry she transforms her affair with Walter Stone into ordinary verse. Ruth Stone's poetry is the ecstasy of memory.

She has gone elsewhere with her love and returned with a poem.

Ruth Stone has lived a life with a suicide. Any fool should know that you never bury the dead, and especially a suicide. So the reader must not be surprised that a secular illuminatus has raised the dead, along with time, and onto a splendid grassy and dirty planet. Walter Stone is her heaven and hell, accompanying her earth time, who has grown with her and kept her at various ages (usually between twenty and forty). He is her fountain of grief and youth. He also keeps alive the places and countries where they once were and every event and intimacy, which have inevitably changed with their formulation in verse. Jorge Luis Borges, quoting his father, said if one wishes to keep a memory intact, don't recall it, for each recollection alters once again the former recollection. But of course Borges knew it is better to remember and change a remembrance than not to recall it and lose it. So through constant remembrance, she has continued the life of the past rather than preserve it unaltered and unobserved in a vault of death. And her contemplation and vivid reexperiencing occur down in the valley and up there in biblical Goshen.

Ruth Stone's enduring love affair with Walter Stone is at the center of her writing. But it would be little, or much less, if it were not, as we have seen, one of the multitudinous experiences and observations in her life. In her poems, everything breeds and feeds on other things, is replaceable and interchangeable. And she remembers them everyplace. When she packs up her clothes, papers, and suns and carts them home, she still carries them to her poor Chinese cottage up high. Li Bai and Du Fu (Li Po and Tu Fu) shared such a hut in the forest of Chengdu, and there they drank and wrote poems. Like a proper Chinese poet-painter, Stone goes higher to dwell in her house on Deep South Mountain where she listens to the haze of the universe tilting on its side toward her orchard.

For four decades I have experienced Ruth Stone as the major poet in our language. She is rich as only a person of authentic poverty can be, opulent in her life and words. She is the English language's secret. That will change, for the secret will out. Yet it will also remain, and it is best that way, that she be undiscovered—except as she is known by each single reader (multitudes of them) who has the chance to discover how the ordinary is extraordinary, how Alexandria resides and resurrects in an apple, a parking lot, a boarding house, on the wallpaper, in the pockets of a cheap second-hand coat, in the arms of her ghost lover with whom she lies in a dingy hotel room, reading Baudelaire.

Works Cited

Barnstone, Aliki, and Willis Barnstone. *A Book of Women Poets from Antiquity to Now*. New York: Schocken, 1992.

Barnstone, Tony, and Willis Barnstone. *Laughing Lost in the Mountains: Poems of Wang Wei*. Hanover: UP of New England, 1991.

Barnstone, Willis. *Sappho and the Greek Lyric Poets*. New York: Schocken, 1988.

Dickinson, Emily. *The Complete Poems of Emily Dickinson*. Ed. Thomas H. Johnson. Boston: Little, 1960.

Eliot, T. S. *Collected Poems 1909–1935*. New York: Harcourt, 1952.

Part III *Reading Ruth Stone*

[Her] voice is as preternaturally responsive to marriage, family, and human solitude as to animals, landscape, and seasons.

–Norman Friedman

10 *The Comedic Art of Ruth Stone*
Diane Wakoski

Dante called his great poem *La Commedia* (only later did he add the word "divine") because "in the conclusion it is prosperous, pleasant, and desirable" and in its style "lax and unpretending," being "written in the vulgar tongue, in which women and children speak" (*OED* 475). Comedy, by the Middle Ages, had become a play with a happy ending. Yet anyone who studies comedy knows that while its effects may be funny, amusing, or pleasant, its underlying purposes include making the audience face more easily the painful nature of reality, often of injustice or inequity. If daily life is sometimes so absurd or painful that we are tempted to think it must be a divine joke, laughed at by the gods, then sometimes we can usefully perceive our pain without grimness or the requirement of tragic conclusions.

Ruth Stone's poetry, like Dante's *Commedia*, gives us the vision of an all-too-human world where the norm is trouble. Paired with it is an acceptance that this is true but that it is *amusing* rather than terrible. In her poem "Being a Woman," she gently mocks the whole condition of half the human race. There is no anger, no bitterness, no grimness. She says,

> You can talk to yourself all you want to.
> After all, you were the only one who ever heard
> What you were saying. And even you forgot
> Those brilliant flashes seen from afar, like Toledo
> Brooding, burning up from the Moorish scimitar.

It has often been said that a biological survival trait is that we forget pain that we've experienced. This allows women to go through the pain of childbirth more than once, or athletes and warriors to train and play difficult and painful games again and again. Ruth Stone introduces that forgetting, ironically, as a kind of combined battling and birthing of female identity. The poem continues:

> Sunk in umber, illuminated at the edges by fitful lightning,
> You subside in the suburbs. Hidden in the shadow of hedges
> You urge your dog to lift his leg on the neighbor's shrubs.
>
> Soldiers are approaching. They are everywhere.
> Behind the lamppost the dog sends unknown messages
> To the unknown. A sensible union of the senses.
> The disengaged ego making its own patterns.
> The voice of the urine saying this has washed away my salt,
> My minerals. My kidneys bless you, defy you, invite you
> To come out and yip with me in the schizophrenic night.
>
> (*S-HC* 75)

In this poem, trouble is the norm. "You can talk to yourself all you want to," she says. "After all, you were the only one who ever heard / What you were saying." Perhaps this sounds as if it could be the fiery introduction to an angry poem. Certainly, there is the awareness of pain, of being ignored by the world both as a person and as a woman. Immediately, though, she follows it with the comic aside—"And even you forgot / Those brilliant flashes seen from afar." In tragedy, the hero cannot see his own part in the trouble until it is too late. The too-lateness is what makes the situation tragic: the hero had the power to prevent the trouble, but his lack of awareness, his blindness, brought everything tumbling down. In comedy, usually the hero also is the unwitting cause of the trouble, but it *is* comedy because he does find this out—before it is too late.

In Ruth Stone's comic poems, tragedy is always averted by immediately seeing and acknowledging responsibility. In "Being a Woman," women forget the pain of having brilliance that is unrecognized by somewhat absurdly accepting their lot. As she says, "You subside into the suburbs" where you walk your dog in a kind of surrealist landscape. Soldiers "are everywhere," and even the dog, her ally, is sending out secret messages encoded in his piss.

She concludes the poem with a comic voice that combines "The voice of the urine," as she calls it, and the disengaged ego, begging the reader to "come out and yip with me in the . . . night." There's danger, there's trouble, but there's relief, if only in the form of pissing when you need to; and being allowed that small thing, you are allowed joy. Rejoicing is possible.

This isn't really satire. It is the comic, what Dante describes as "in the conclusion . . . prosperous, pleasant, and desirable." It is not the irony of tragedy; rather, it is the wit, the making fun of one's inevitable condition, painful but not deadly. It is not really stoicism, but it's not Pollyanna-acceptance, either. Comedy is for the release of pain, not by laughing at it but by looking away, distracting oneself—in amusement. In *Anatomy of an Illness*, Norman Cousins talks about how he conquered a painful illness by watching Marx Brothers movies and other comedies, which every few hours would help relieve the pain. He distracted himself with laughter while the healing process went on.

In Ruth Stone's poem, there is an unendurable but insoluble pain: that of being a woman. Nothing can change that. But the woman in the poem distracts herself with another pain, one that can be eliminated: a full bladder. She walks her dog, and in the relief the dog feels, which she can identify with, there is the freedom from one pressing pain that momentarily, at least, frees, releases/ distracts her from the inevitable one of "being a woman."

Reading the poem this way illustrates that the comedy of Ruth Stone is more personal than political. Politically, the message of the poem might be considered irresponsible. Yet, what the poem seems to be is a comic and personal response to a world where the heroine has acknowledged that the only power she can have is through her vision. Unlike Dante, she does not think her vision should have the authority of church or state: thus, the poems work like lyric poems rather than political or social dramas. They are personal comedies with their "happy endings" consisting in the poet's being alive and well to say what she thinks and feels and to show us she is continually rather amused by it all.

It is not that there is no dramatic irony in Ruth Stone's comedic vision, but rather that no one is required to die or to be exiled, tortured, punished, or ravaged before the truth is known. Human life is not a tragedy to Ruth Stone, though she acknowledges both its seriousness and its pain. In her poem "The Plan," she talks about a lifetime of problem solving.

> I said to myself, do you have a plan?
> And the answer was always, no, I have no plan.
> Then I would say to myself, you must think of one.
> But what happened went on, chaotic with necessary pain.

The problems, the pains of everyday life she calls "necessary pain," a lovely, efficient phrase, neither masochistic nor sadistic, not so much stoical as matter-of-fact. She goes on, describing her life:

> During the winter the dogs dug moles from their runs
> And rolled them blind on the frozen road.
> Then the crossbills left at the equinox.
> All this time I tried to think of a plan,
> Something to bring the points together.
> I saw that we move in a circle
> But I was wordless in the field.
> The smell of green steamed, everything shoved,
> But I folded my hands and sat on the rocks.
> Here I am, I said, with my eyes.
> When they have fallen like marbles from their sockets,
> What will become of this? And then I remembered
> That there were young moles in my mind's eye,
> Whose pink bellies shaded to mauve plush,
> Whose little dead snouts sparkled with crystals of frost;
> And it came to me, the blind will be leading the blind.
>
> (*S-HC* 99)

I suppose you could read this poem as elegiac; certainly there is some of the power of the lyric about it, as all of Ruth Stone's poems contain great lyricism. But they are not primarily lyrics. And this is not an elegy. It is a comic poem concluding with her amusing/ amused thought about the irony of living according to plan, whether you have a plan or not.

Certainly, I will not deprive the good reader of many other interpretations of this fine, ambiguous poem; it reminds me a great deal of Richard Wilbur's "The Beautiful Changes," but my point here is to show that Ruth Stone's poetry offers no other clear set of reading possibilities than the comedic. For it is not satirical in purpose; it is not a lyric song; it is not so much narrative as personal; and it is not so personal that it is confessional or dramatic. What really links all of Ruth Stone's poems is a clear, continuing, and lucid comic vision of the world—one that allows her to take pain in her stride. It is, in the translation of Dante's words about his own *Commedia*, poetry whose "conclusion . . . is prosperous, pleasant, and desirable." Ruth Stone is a poet opening the door to an American comedic verse.

Work Cited

The Compact Edition of the Oxford English Dictionary. Vol. 1. Oxford: Oxford UP, 1971.

11 *Ruth Stone's Magic Mixture*
Diana O'Hehir

When I thought about Ruth Stone's poetry, I found I was remembering most vividly the hilarious humor and the wrenching sense of loss, occurring, side by side, in the same poem. I wanted to write about this double aspect of Stone's art and set myself the task of exploring that space, somewhere out in the Milky Way, where those two parallel lines of emotion meet for her.

I asked myself two questions: how does Stone accomplish this fusion of tragedy and comedy, and what are its effects on the reader? I ended up with several answers, but the ones that interested me most involved the poems where she uses an ostensibly comic frame as a setting for tragic material, a frame where the verse structure of the poem, its skeleton or form, uses rhythms, rhymes, sound clusters, and words that are usually recognized as comic.

"The Tree," for instance, is one of Stone's most wrenching poems, a searing depiction of grief and loss at a husband's suicide. But the rhythm is the singsong one of a jingle. The poem begins:

> I was a child when you married me
> A child I was when I married you
> But I was a regular midwest child,
> And you were a Jew.
>
> (*S-HC* 61)

Here's a familiar cadence, that of a number of works that all of us have rattling around in the backs of our memories—"The Owl and the Pussycat," first of all: Edward Lear's "The Owl and the Pussycat went to sea / In a beautiful pea-green boat." After that there is Mother Goose: "Where are you going to, my pretty maid?," or

"How many miles to Babylon?"—I'm sure everyone will think of other examples. The repetitions and inversions ("I was a child . . . A child I was . . .") are also typical of those verses we had read to us when we were too small to object ("O lovely Pussy! O Pussy, my love . . .").

If that last remark seems equivocal, it is intentionally so. Personally, I loved those verses and now think that they often rose to become true poetry, but surely in these grim times we realize the veiled threat behind each one. What designs did the pussycat have on the owl? And what designs had that overly solicitous young man on the maid? The poem about the road to Babylon is now generally recognized as being one about the road to death. These nursery poems thus convey a double message, at the same time funny and terrifying, and when Stone borrows their rhythms she is immediately establishing a double comic-tragic course for her poem.

Stone is also doing a number of other complicated things: she is provoking in us the nostalgia of the familiar, reminding us of rhythms and work patterns that we have been taught to consider funny; at the same time, she is reawakening the subliminal fears that for many of us accompany those patterns.

"The Song of Absinthe Granny" is about a hectic life of uncontrolled search and disaster; it very suitably borrows its rhythms from another Mother Goose poem, "Old Mother Hubbard":

> Those were high kick summers,
> It was bald galled fun .
>
>> ("Absinthe Granny," *S-HC* 87)
>
> She went to the baker
> To get him some bread . . .
>
>> ("Old Mother Hubbard")

The continuing rhythmic and rhyming parallels are very close, with longer lines occurring at the beginning of each poem. Threat, death, chaos are again implicit in the model just as they are in Stone's poem: "And when she returned / The poor dog was dead . . ." Mother Hubbard's dog revives, and so do the poem's children, who, although thought to be dead, are really "under the shed"; but a husband goes to town and never reappears.

Still another nursery rhyme provides the pattern for "Procedure." "Here is old Bessie," the poem commences; it continues in subsequent stanzas with "Here she is squeezed"; "Here comes the surgeon." The model, of course, is that scariest nursery rhyme of all, "Here comes a candle to light you to bed / Here comes a chopper to chop off your head," a suitable background for a poem about an old lady who is sent to the hospital and

> . . . chop for chop
> and loin for loin, all her grits and greens
> turned into tasty cuts . . .
>
> (*S-HC* 35)

"Salt" is a mysterious journey into terror, discovery, and disillusion:

> In the hourglass
> It came to pass
> I returned from where I died
> With my funeral veil
> And my fairy tale
> And the tears I never cried.
>
> (*S-HC* 96)

These jumpy rhythms echo, among other rambles, the Mikado's song about the punishment fitting the crime:

> On a cloth untrue
> With a twisted cue
> And elliptical billiard balls . . .
>
> (Gilbert and Sullivan)

Again the model is funny, enough, and bloodthirsty, plenty.

Finally, although with trepidation, I'm going to add "Orange Poem Praising Brown" to this survey. The poem is probably tragic only to another poet. But it's a more serious poem than it may initially appear to be, and I love it inordinately. It starts out with our old friend and enemy, the quick brown typewriter fox, a ridiculous model that is threatening insofar as any tedious learning process is threatening; it twists and turns this typewriter exercise throughout the poem, concluding finally with disaster for the poet.

In each of these examples, the frame draws its comic direction not only from its likeness to nursery verses with all they evoke but also from its own rhymes. Triple rhymes and rhymes between words with wildly variant spellings are traditionally seen as funny in English; we associate them with Ogden Nash, with Gilbert and Sullivan, with Dorothy Parker. And so many of Stone's rhymes are traditionally funny ones: in "Tree," "unity," "trinity," and "will to be" are comic signals.

This kind of rhyming is constant for her. Thus, "Absinthe Granny" gives us "furry," "story," and "tarry" and "sipper" and "nipper"; "Procedure" and "Orange Poem," which aren't systematically rhymed, produce near-rhymes and assonances: "rustle" and "gristle" in "Procedure," "lenses," "links," "lips," and "lousy" for "Orange Poem." Sounds that are awkward and therefore traditionally funny abound: "shuffled" and "snuffled," "rah" and "raved," "mop" and "string" (*S-HC* 86–88), "wink" (*S-HC* 35), "thud" (*S-HC* 96).

The comic-threatening framework that we have been examining surrounds a tragic narrative: in three of my five examples, the narrative is desperately tragic. Tragic subject and tragicomic form become married in complicated ways that depend partly on the form's dual nature but also on elements within the subject matter.

This subject matter, like its frame, is dual; that is, it asks for several simultaneous responses or for sudden revisions of attitude. It accomplishes these things by broad shifts in association, by jumps in subject. Thus, within one poem, "Salt," the reader must leap from a world of modern poetic dislocation, "the bell toll of a clang," to a fairy tale world, "the land of nowhere," and from there to traditional myth, "the hanging tree," then to religious myth, "Jehovah," and so on through the debased world of "too fat," to end with an ordinary prosaic wisdom: "We all die / On the down side" (*S-HC* 95).

For me, the most interesting of this series of shifts, occurring in all the poems I've examined, is a high point in four of them where either sex or religion (or in two cases both at once) are referred to in startling and story-stopping ways. When this happens it's a focus for the poem, a turning point.

The beginning of "The Tree" is a chatty examination of the writer's family background. In verse four, the emotional tempo changes:

> Then you took me in with your bony knees,
> And it wasn't them that I wanted to please—
> It was Jesus Christ that I had to squeeze;
> Oh, glorious you.

Surely this is one of the most daring fusions of sexuality and religion in literature. From this point on, the poem is specific in its identification of the hanged husband with the crucified Christ and of the wife's love with a Christian convert's love:

> Love and touch and unity.
> Parting and joining; the trinity
> Was flesh, the mind and the will to be.
> The world grew through me like a tree.
>
> (*S-HC* 61)

All of this passion and pain is set forth in the ridiculous triple rhymes of Gilbert and Sullivan.

"Salt" again begins on an ambiguous note ("the land of nowhere"), then it shifts into religion/sex/threat:

> No woman is fair sang the grass,
> They eat up the men, sang the grass
> And the mist of the hanging tree
> Smiled in the beard of Jehovah . . .
>
> (*S-HC* 95)

And later on in the poem,

> . . . we'll let you look in
> At the sorcerer's virginal house of skin,
> Where no woman goes . . .
>
> (*S-HC* 96)

A primitive tribal religion is implied by these lines: it's a different religion from the more familiar Christianity of "The Tree," but an equally alarming one for the reader, equally defeating for the poem's persona.

Three words—alert, alarm, awaken—cover the reaction Stone gets from this kind of startling of the reader and realigning of the poem. The reader is alerted and alarmed; the persona in the poem is awakened to special understanding; the poem itself is awakened and repositioned, sometimes several times. After the beginning of "Orange Poem," with the tedious typing exercise, comes an ear-popping sexuality, nasty instructions from the poem itself: "Praise my loose hung dangle . . . / Tell me about myself in oral fragments" (*S-HC* 29).

Sex or religion or both serve the purpose of shaking the poem up, shaking up the reader. Ultimately, I think Ruth Stone's art in these strong poems consists in doing that over and over. She lures the reader in with the familiar rhythms of childhood, promises a pattern that the reader can join in on and follow along with, and then pulls the entire structure out from under the feet.

For this reader, at least, the result is that I am glued to the page. I have a tendency to write the poem along with the poet, to try to get one line ahead of her, to anticipate what is happening. Because Stone's poetry is usually either rhymed or assonant, I temporarily have the pleasant illusion that I can do this. Then, just when I'm happily participating in the creative process, I'm yanked alert by a radical, perhaps an idiotic departure. A reader enjoys feeling participation, but most readers like much better to be surprised, startled, and made to follow gasping at the heels of an agile guide. And that's the energy and exercise that Ruth Stone's poetry provides.

After all, what else can you expect from a poet who describes spring in these unconventional terms:

> Plants, animals, swollen with excess
> are straining to keep their balance.
> Two hot days and the population explodes off the circuits,
> jams the sewers.
> Afterbirth reeks in the swamps, gluts the rivers.
> And everything that lived through last year
> is out fattening itself, eating the babies.
>
> (*S-HC* 24)

Work Cited

Gilbert, W. S., and Arthur Sullivan. "The Mikado's Song." London: Chappell, 1949.

12 "The Wife's Went Bazook"

Comedic Feminism in the Poetry of Ruth Stone
Kevin Clark

In the tradition of American naturalism, the more recent poems of Ruth Stone's *Second-Hand Coat: Poems New and Selected* (1987) are always sociologically acute and often thin on hope. Stone's darkly feminist work employs humor to render the lives of people pushed to the margins of society by economics and gender bias. Encountering one of the relatives or friends who populate the pages of her poetry can be like encountering one of the squalid, unsheltered human beings who populate the streets of our towns and cities. Admittedly, one of Stone's protagonists is frequently funny while the homeless person rarely is. And we appreciate the wisdom of her loopy creation while we avert our eyes from the deranged stare of the insanitary man or woman. But there is more to the parallel.

On first reading *Second-Hand Coat*, one can mistake Stone's characters for simply being cartoon-daft in the American tradition. It's true that they are usually unequipped to live adequately in the real world. Two or three bubbles off plumb, they unwittingly—and thus comically—demonstrate wisdom from time to time. And while they are, finally, without the kind of psychological strength that affords both poise and flexibility, many manage to form a worldview that enables them to get by. It would thus be a mistake to see all of Stone's characters as cartoon innocents merely happening upon smarts during their helpless travails. Like many of the homeless, they have been driven to the margins of human existence by an inability to sustain normalcy in an adversarial locale. Most survive; some don't; all suffer.

And yet Stone's characters are not truly homeless; rather they are usually women devising methods for maintaining an eccentric balance within both a world of quotidian domestic chores and a patriarchy devaluing them as people. Some of Stone's most memorable characters are women who have tried to develop a proactive tool for surviving, especially by creating their own oddball universe of perceptions and rules that counter the dominant but equally bizarre network of forces that constitute early- and mid-twentieth-century American civilization. I'm interested primarily in Stone's comic portraiture of relatives and friends—Aunt Maud, Mrs. Dubosky, the Masons, Ida, Absinthe Granny—in which she has forged her own kind of comedic feminism, employing the colloquial, sometimes rural dialects of lower- and middle-class white America to help depict methods for coping.

While we first laugh at these women because we recognize their language, obsessions, and even small successes, each poem's comic calculations are complex because each also carries a kind of compassion for the women—and even for a culture that has rendered such self-defeating dynamics. While theorists are in endless conflict about what triggers human laughter, we probably laugh on reading Stone's portraiture because each poem bears closely upon some fearful fragment of our own experience. In fact, we recognize the very world that conspires against women like Aunt Maud and Absinthe Granny. We come to understand that there's a direct relationship between their behavior and the world, which has itself gone berserk—at least in Stone's eyes. We're surprised that these unstable characters have the capacity for knowing truth, or even for making a reasonably clear utterance, for that matter. We recognize a cartooned form of ourselves in that world, cartoons who really could exist—and do. Some of her characters happen upon transient moments of enlightenment, some tragically regress from a hard-earned entropy to an increasingly dazed neurasthenia, while still others create their own vengeful personalities that leave them dominant but often sadly alone in the micro-universe of their domiciles.

Aunt Maud is perhaps Stone's benchmark character because she maintains a kind of zero-sum game with the relentless demands of housework, clothing, and her husband, who, we can surmise, she perceives as almost alien. Because "How Aunt Maud Took to Being a Woman" is a brief, tightly controlled piece with a punch line, I quote it in its entirety:

> A long hill sloped down to Aunt Maud's brick house.
> You could climb an open stairway up the back
> to a plank landing where she kept her crocks of wine.
> I got sick on stolen angelfood cake and green wine
> and slept in her feather bed for a week.
> Nobody said a word. Aunt Maud just shifted
> the bottles. Aunt's closets were all cedar lined.
> She used the same pattern for her house dresses—
> thirty years. Plain ugly, closets full of them,
> you could generally find a new one cut and laid
> out on her sewing machine. She preserved,
> she canned. Her jars climbed the basement walls.
> She was a vengeful housekeeper. She kept the blinds
> pulled down in the parlor. Nobody really walked
> on her hardwood floors. You lived in the kitchen.
> Uncle Cal spent a lot of time on the back porch
> waiting to be let in.
>
> (S-HC 32)

At first, we understand the joke is on poor Uncle Cal, a husband who is in an orbit so distant from Maud's private planet as to be exiled. Maud can be nurturing; as a girl, the narrator is grateful for her aunt's acceptance of her own youthful misfortune. We see Maud's idiosyncracies as comically endearing, but after the first appreciative gloss we take from this poem, we may begin to realize that Maud is also exiled, and not simply from intimacy. In her compulsiveness she may have Uncle Cal's number, but something else is missing. An inveterate organizer and housekeeper as well as a dully practical and redundant seamstress, Maud is effectively cut off from a balanced range of human pleasures. There's no sense of beauty in her life, only a raging contest for order.

Maud doesn't know how to relax because she is fighting the inanity of her gender role as delineated for most American women previous to the women's revolution. Her eccentric obsession with preparation, conservation, and preservation are indicative of someone who would relax only at risk of losing out to the forces of entropy. Of course, most adults experience similar pressures at different times, but most men could always leave the house, enter the culture, "do" something, and return to the house without knowing the tyranny of demands on the housekeeper. Meanwhile, the relentless forces of dirt and disorder can wear down the housekeeper's psyche. What else begins to emerge but the threat of death? Death from failure as the manager of the home; death from the impossible battles against time, the enemy of all homes; death from strangulation that comes from an inability to catch one's breath, from being smothered by a repetitive work life, and finally, perhaps a deathly fear not only that this life is killing in its endless tasks but also that it is the only life she can possibly have. The irony is that Maud, like many women in her shoes, represses these fears by working even harder.

The poem's punch line supplies a comic victory. Maud's the one who controls the home, and she can't let Uncle Cal in for several reasons: obviously, he is going to consume those canned foods and mess up the house. Not only is he a man, a creature of the off-limits world beyond the home, but he is also a carrier, a symbol of the entropic world in which energy wastes itself into disorder. Maud's act of temporarily exiling him is a kind of futile stay against the next working day, the next sweeping, canning. We know to laugh because old Cal is probably quite useless in Maud's domain, and she'll be damned if she's going to let him muck things up if she doesn't have to.

So Stone's poem is unapologetically feminist in its depiction of the self-defeating, skewed values of a patriarchal society. The title humorously but clearly announces the poem's sociopolitical intent. "How Aunt Maud Took to Being a Woman" is at first funny because Maud's solution to the female problem of gender role and identity is familiar, eccentric, and, to a certain extent, winning. Aunt Maud may be slightly touched, but she manages, and with some degree of power. Maud's the champion of her own domain—a survivor gone a bit bonkers, but a survivor nonetheless. Stone, however, doesn't let us stay satisfied with Maud's predicament. After the laughter dies down, we realize Maud has sacrificed aesthetics, tranquility, and intimacy to achieve what she's needed. We care deeply about Aunt Maud, but we're left with images of a human being trapped in a manic and incessant perseverance.

Still, several of Stone's subjects don't make out as well as Aunt Maud. In "What Can You Do?," Mrs. Dubosky has developed her own methods for dealing with a battering husband, an ungrateful son, two ungrateful daughters-in-law, mortgage payments, and the trauma known as marriage. Like Maud, she is careful and persevering: she loves her grandchildren, always carries sharpened pencils in her apron for them, and constantly searches out wastebaskets for stamps, which she steams off envelopes for the boys' collection. Buoying her perseverance, however, isn't so much optimism as a kind of fatalism:

> Mrs. Dubosky is paying on a trailer.
> She can't retire until she's paid off the seven thousand.
> She's sixty-two.
> Mrs. Dubosky says, "We'll see."
>
> (*S-HC* 7)

Mrs. Dubosky knows not to expect too much; like Maud, her life is circumscribed by the culture's limiting set of presumptions. Her new daughter-in-law lives with her in the trailer while her son drives his semi cross-country. The old daughter-in-law managed to get the old house. Mrs. Dubosky makes it clear she has to make exceptions for the marital failures of her son, from whom not much can be expected. She would, of course, never think to question her devotion to family. In loving them, she simply knows she must succumb to their inevitably troubled goings-on.

Stone's language mimics Mrs. Dubosky's fatalism. The narrator's tale is interspersed with quotations from Mrs. Dubosky, both speakers rendered in a series of declarative sentences piling one upon another without a stanza break for fifty-eight lines. The poem almost reads like an absurdist interview or feature article, its humor arising from the fact that its subject is not exciting or typically distinctive enough to warrant such journalistic focus. And we also laugh at the burlesque of this record, that is, the sheer unstoppable onslaught of bad news, the ongoing material banality, and the inference that it's all inevitable because it is inherited:

> Mrs. Dubosky wears other people's old tennis shoes.
> Chemicals in the cleaning water eat right through them.
> She's got a bad leg.
> Her mother's legs were bad. They had to be amputated.
> While her mother was in the hospital,
> her father's colostomy quit working and he got a blockage.
>
> (S-HC 7–8)

All of this is told directly, in even tones, as if all were to be expected, as if nothing could surprise Mrs. Dubosky. Surely, more bad news is just around the corner. And, in order to depict faithfully her subject's resignation, the narrator employs a white, lower-middle-class dialect ("he got a blockage") intended to mimic Mrs. Dubosky's way of speaking.

But nothing in the poem is as sadly comic as the last nineteen lines, almost all spoken by Mrs. Dubosky and all devoted to the subject of marriage, which is clearly the primary source of her problems. Reminiscent of the pub scene in "The Waste Land," this passage is a sharply synthesized moment of colloquial speech, storytelling, and wish projection, designed to give us a glimpse of the small happiness Mrs. Dubosky dreams after:

> "Marriage," says Mrs. Dubosky. "You know how it is.
> I had just had the baby.
> My husband was after me all the time.
> You know, physical.
> Oh, he slapped me but that's not what I mean.
> My mother came over and she said,
> 'What's the matter with you?'
> You know, the eyebags was down on the cheeks.
> I says, 'He's always after me,'
> and she says, 'You're gonna come home.'
> The judge said he'd never seen a case that bad.
> You know what he called him? He said,
> 'You're nothing but a beast.'"
> Mrs. Dubosky isn't sure. She says,
> "What can you do?"

When she retires, she tells me,
she's going to get a dog. One of those nice little ones.
"When you rub them on the belly
they lie back limp," she says, "and just let you."

(*S-HC* 8)

Where Maud took control of her life in her own idiosyncratic
manner, Mrs. Dubosky—always plaintive, tentative, and fundamen-
tally kind—finds lasting happiness beyond her grasp, in an imagined
future, in the form of a grateful and obedient dog. She figures her
husband may or may not have been "a beast," but now she'd clearly
replace him with a different companion, one who isn't dangerous,
merely malleable. Unwilling to condemn anyone, even an abusive
husband, Mrs. Dubosky temporarily sequesters herself from the
belligerent forces of love in a man's world by retiring temporarily
to her imagination.

Thus, like Aunt Maud, Mrs. Dubosky does retain her mental
health. But in several of Stone's poems from *Second-Hand Coat*, the
sanity of the central characters is in greater danger. In "Sunday,"
the Masons are thrilled by death; though Stone's focus here isn't
exclusively upon a woman, many of the cultural problems she identifies still adhere. The fear of a paralyzing life, of a deathly stasis, of
time spent doing little meaningful work, of a retirement spent
waiting for demise, all this sends the Masons out to their weekly
hospital visit as if to church:

> Long antiseptic Sundays, tubes of interstitial fluids,
> bed pans, strangers lying in metal beds.
> They got off on face masks.
> They liked to press their thumbs on your wrist
> and feel your pulse.

(*S-HC* 26)

The death-in-life syndrome exhibited by Maud emerges here, too.
Rather than defer their fears by losing themselves in work, though,
the Masons give themselves over to the failing flesh of others. The
subconscious fear of the boring, deadly life is circumvented by a
fascination with the actual physical dying of others. And Stone ups
the ironic ante by placing all the action in the past tense, allowing

for the clear possibility that the Masons themselves may eventually have become the very people they came to see.

"Sunday" is dark comedy, for sure, but darker still is "The Latest Hotel Guest Walks over Particles That Revolve in Seven Other Dimensions Controlling Latticed Space" in which a woman stays in a hotel room for two mentally degenerating weeks. Here she imagines the micrometric elements of public and private horrors, including

> . . . Vietnam,
> the Cuban crisis, little difficulties
> with the Shah . . .

as well as "room 404" that

> probably now contains the escaped molecules,
> radiation photons and particulate particles
> of the hair and skin of all its former guests.
>
> (*S-HC* 40)

The poem is no knee-slapper, but it is comic in its deft play on popular physics. The guest has become obsessed with the science of entropy in which energy spins destructively into disorder. She is a woman whose imagination is passing from a sensitized state of empathy to an increasingly chaotic neurosis. She imagines all the smallest particles of all the former guests of her room forming an android, which she can hear

> . . . among her blouses and slacks
> and she knows at this moment it is, at last,
> counting from ten to zero.
>
> (*S-HC* 41)

If "zero" is the point at which the last strings of the balanced life give way, the hotel guest may in fact also be the subject of "Being a Woman," a tautly comic poem about why a woman may talk to herself: "After all, you were the only one who ever heard / What you were saying" (*S-HC* 75). Once again, the title announces the poem's sociopolitical intent unequivocally. Stone's genius here is in capturing the bizarre and contradictory but perhaps too common state of mind that can come of being stuck in a woman's gender role. On one hand, there are freedoms in not being taken seriously. Unfortunately, because some women internalize the attendant idea that they are not *worth* being taken seriously, it is difficult for them to exploit the small freedom to act as if their behavior doesn't matter. Walking her dog in the suburbs, this protagonist doesn't begin to identify with the atomized visitors of a hotel room but rather with all the dogs in the neighborhood. As the woman's dog marks its territory, Stone's language is neither colloquial nor scientific; each line is almost formal in its strange invocation:

> The disengaged ego making its own patterns.
> The voice of the urine saying this has washed away my salt,
> My minerals. My kidneys bless you, defy you, invite you
> To come out and yip with me in the schizophrenic night.
>
> (*S-HC* 75)

Identifying with the voice of the yipping dog, the woman invites company. But who does she intend? Perhaps the other women who have been unheard all their lives? Or perhaps the men who haven't heard the women speaking? Either way, the poem suggests the human yip is futile and the only result is a state of schizophrenia in which the mind is split between a freedom and an irrelevancy.

"Bazook" is more conventionally funny than "The Latest Hotel Guest" and "Being a Woman," but the poem's protagonist, Ida, actually does go completely out of her mind and must be institutionalized. Poor Ida's "went bazook" because the old house she willfully leaves for a new Florida home was as psychological an edifice as it was physical. If Aunt Maud's house was a prison of sorts, at least it was her prison, controlled and run by Maud. And as we know by virtue of Uncle Cal's residency on the back porch, Maud's home kept out forces that weren't especially benevolent. Apparently, the same could be said for Ida's longtime domicile. Ida's tragic mistake lies in her ignorance of the value of the old place:

> Fred and Ida.
> They had a lovely little house.
> For two years all that two talked
> Was, wait till we get to Florida,
> Wait till we get to Florida.
> It's going to be this and that.

Then finally they sold
And moved to Clearwater, Fla.
And built this place.
And the next thing we hear,
The wife's went bazook!

(*S-HC* 84)

Ida loses her mind because she's left the old house; that is, she's given up perhaps the most important check against the forces of lunacy. Though she moves into a brand new home, she has effectively become homeless. Her new environment can never replace the deeply familiar walls and reassuring artifacts of the old. Like so many of Stone's protagonists who are isolated and displaced, Ida waged a contest for normalcy. It is a difficult contest to win, though, because the culture's parameters of normalcy are rigid, restrictive, and usually male-defined. There's very little room for idiosyncracy.

We laugh at this tragic tale because it's told in the astonished voice of a neighbor who can't figure out what went wrong. We laugh because *we* know what went wrong. To a greater or lesser extent, we've been there. We're there now. We all camouflage our freakishness, and we all learn how to defend against the constricting idiosyncracies of civilization. And one of our proactive defenses is the same one employed by this neighbor or the Masons or Mrs. Dubosky: a capacity for astonishment. Transcendence sometimes comes at the expense of others, and often we are lifted out of our own problems—or ennui—by the seemingly fresh and amazing difficulties of others. Such a stance is proactive because it is as offensive as it is defensive; it requires that we first see these characters as inferior. In "How Aunt Maud Took to Being a Woman," we initially laugh at Uncle Cal's impotence. Even Aunt Maud sees him as unworthy of entry, beneath the distaff standards of the home. But then we begin to see Aunt Maud for what she is—sadly eccentric. And finally, upon further contemplation, we can begin to see that we, too, are eccentric, perhaps secretly so, but also perhaps not that far from Maud in our peculiarities. After all, how would we behave if we had been put in Maud's worn shoes?

Stone is clearly ironic in her use of humor because, while she suggests we laugh at others, she does so with didactic intent. She knows that we will realize a single hard fact: that we could just as easily be the subjects of someone else's laughter. (If she were Irish, she might have each of us saying, "There but for the grace of God go I.") As we read and laugh we forget ourselves momentarily, only to return to Stone's underlying premise: that domestic life in a patriarchal civilization can be pulverizing, that this civilization entraps us as well. Serious consideration of Stone's poetry can lead to a healthy dose of humility.

And unlike the fathers of American naturalism—Norris, Dreiser, Crane—Ruth Stone is not completely beholden to the doctrines of fatalism. She is nearly unrivaled in her humanitarian insistence; her sense of humor is founded on the notion that we are all both absurd and worthy of love, and she wields her humor against a life that can be crushing in its redundancy and a culture that can be crushing in its rigidity. Stone's humor is the one romantic strand in her work. Laughing is the last redemption, and while we may laugh in amazement at the trials of others, her comic focus ultimately points to ourselves. Stone's poetry is prescriptive in its suggestion that we maintain at least as comic a perception of ourselves as we do of anything else in life while we simultaneously sustain an awareness of the forces that destroy the human spirit. And no poem better reflects this humanitarian notion than the uniquely romantic rhyme "The Song of Absinthe Granny."

Absinthe Granny is nobody's fool: she knows she's crazy and she may hit the bottle, yet she's hung on, not simply for the sake of her kids, but because for her—unlike Ida—the alternative is unacceptable. She's the archetypal female survivor: Ruth Stone's version of an ideal Everywoman straight from Maud's rural neck of the woods. She tells her life story in an unbroken eighty-three-line column, using a velocitous nursery rhyme to comic effect. In this poem, in fact, Stone's language draws not only on children's rhythm and rhyme but also on the crazy and quick associative turns of some children's tales, thereby mimicking Granny's nuttiness.

Unlike Aunt Maud, Absinthe Granny is aware of her own mental problems, admitting at one point, "I couldn't see for my head was thatched" (*S-HC* 87). She is also aware of two salient truths: that the cause of her troubles is in part connected to the demands of motherhood, housekeeping, and husband, and that the path to survival involves making the best of what she's been given, including mental illness. With the house a mess from "Diapers and panty-shirts and yolk of eggs" (86), Granny's frantic regimen leads to hallucinations—but she simply makes them work for her:

> One day in the mirror I saw my stringy legs
> And I looked around
> And saw string on the floor,
> And string on the chair
> And heads like wasps' nest
> Full of stringy hair.
> "Well," I said, "if you have string, knit.
> Knit something, don't just sit."
>
> (*S-HC* 86)

Eventually her husband—inert and as dimly informed of his wife's inner world as Uncle Cal was of Maud's—tells her how good their life is. Granny has an understandably murderous fantasy but keeps on "knitting" through the chaos:

> So I got the rifle out
> To shoot him through the head.
> But he went on smiling and sitting
> And I looked around for a piece of string
> To do some knitting.
> Then I picked at the tiling
> and the house fell down.

The last two lines of this passage borrow, of course, from "The Yellow Wallpaper," but unlike the protagonist of Charlotte Perkins Gilman's story, Granny doesn't dissolve.

With Maud's type of perseverance and her own unique and steady optimism, Granny sees herself through the time of motherhood—and, significantly, with the passing of motherhood and the death of her husband, Granny is no longer subject to hallucinations:

> Well, all that's finished,
> It's all been done.
> Those were high kick summers,
> It was bald galled fun.

Now the daft time's over
And the string is spun.

(*S-HC* 87)

She has no regrets. As she makes clear in the last lines of the poem, she still takes her absinthe, and despite her age, she's not likely to give in to melancholy or despair:

Those were long hot summers,
Now the sun won't tarry.
My birds have flocked,
And I'm old and wary.
I'm old and worn and a cunning sipper,
And I'll outlive every little nipper.
And with what's left I'm chary,
And with what's left I'm chary.

(*S-HC* 88)

Despite Absinthe Granny's drive and upbeat voice, the last word of the poem, repeated for effect, makes it clear that even in her most positivist work, Stone is not a believer in a sentimental and sweeping victory of good over evil. "The Song of Absinthe Granny" is obviously parodic, made clear by the compelling first two lines: "Among some hills there dwelt in parody / A young woman; me." Even in a parody, Stone is not going to give in to the unrealistic hope of a markedly better world. Granny is a drinker, she's been crazy, she survived, and she knows not to trust life as a gracious provider. She may have the capacity for enjoyment, but while the archaic connotations of the term "chary" suggest Granny is dear unto herself, the word also carries a much less optimistic connotation: that she knows to be cautious and watchful in a world that can collapse around her.

Melding comedy and catastrophe is risky business, and it is not difficult to imagine that the world has once or twice collapsed around Stone herself. Rendering the quirks of aunts and friends isn't the only comic risk Stone takes, nor is it the most startling. No other poet I can think of has succeeded in using the comic voice while writing about the death by suicide of her own husband, yet Stone does so in one in five of the newer poems in *Second-Hand*

Coat. This topic is difficult enough to write about, but in one extraordinary poem, Stone is actually funny about it.

The comedy of "Curtains" is, of course, pointed, dark, even an exposition of anger. (And like Plath, she's quite cognizant of her black-comedic method: "Every day I dig you up," she says in "Habit," "You are my joke, / My poem" [*S-HC* 63].) But "Curtains" is closely related to all of her other comedic poems in its defense of idiosyncratic behavior, which here is actually cited as a reason for living. The narrator, aching for her dead husband, declares, "I become my Aunt Virginia / proud but weak in the head" (*S-HC* 15). And while she's not as unsettled as Absinthe Granny, the narrator tells two stories of her own unusual behavior. In the first, she has a wild, hysterical exchange with her screaming landlord, "Mr. Tempesta," who refuses to let her keep her new cats. Of course, his nerves are shot, too; after she shouts and throws books, he relents and they cry together. The second story follows in the last five lines of the poem. Addressing her husband, the narrator delivers this rising comic anecdote and, then, abrupt comic reversal:

> I want to dig you up and say, look,
> it's like the time, remember,
> when I ran into our living room naked
> to get rid of that fire inspector.
>
> See what you miss by being dead?
>
> (*S-HC* 15)

It's as if the narrator says, this is who I am: I may be a bit unusual but I'm damned smart, too. I know what I'm doing. Weren't the incongruities of my personality, the whimsy, the foibles, the fantasia—weren't they rich enough for you? We may laugh at the last line not simply because it's ridiculous to tell the dead what they're missing, but also because we see, behind the transparent mask of humor, the face of a justifiably resentful woman—and we react to the stunning synthesis: in a courageous turn, Stone has made herself one of her own idiosyncratic creations. "Curtains" makes it easier for us to understand the driving empathy that infuses her comic voice.

I once heard the poet Brenda Hillman say that the most effective writing teacher helps the student to recognize and exploit what is idiosyncratically best in the student's poetic voice. Hillman's assumption is that the most effective voice of the writer emanates from that part of the imagination usually kept under wraps for the sake of good form. Certainly, some of the best poets of our recent past— Lowell, Ginsberg, Plath—*have* unmasked themselves, have revealed the inner fusion of oddness and insight that comprises their genius. They have turned inward to the idiosyncratic quick, which is most honestly self-identifying. And yet even these poets are only rarely funny.

While any romantic tone of Stone's poetry is clearly muted by her lowered expectations of the world, she is in the end a comedic advocate of sorts. Stone's sense of comic portraiture helps to make a case for the oddball, especially for wounded and eccentric women. Such an advocate role can be a dangerous business for the poet because, in this case, she takes the risk that her audience will recognize their own secret abnormalities and, thus, turn away from the poem. But Ruth Stone is an example of the rarest poet who intuits that the most idiosyncratically resonant aspects of her own voice are her own empowering refusal to adopt the conventions of others, which she knows can lead to a fast death, and her uncanny ability to see and depict the domestic foibles of women. She is riled by the quotidian pursuit of normalcy in a world that is cold and oppressive as well as downright weird itself, and she reacts by burlesquing its victims in order to highlight not only its grinding routine but its callous demands that we ascribe to social roles that threaten our soundness of mind.

13 *Violence and War, Ethics and Erotics*

Ruth Stone's "Miraculous Translations"
Elyse Blankley

> The antiwar and human rights poems
> are processed in the white room.
> Everyone in there wears sterile gauze.
> These poems go for a lot.
> No one wants to mess up.
> There's expensive equipment involved,
> The workers have to be heavy,
> very heavy.
> These poems are packaged in cement.
> You frequently hear them drop with a dull thud.
> —Ruth Stone, "Some Things You'll Need to Know
> Before You Join the Union"

Ruth Stone is an anomaly among American poets: she loves heavy themes but loathes heavy poems. Shunning the solemn aesthetics of an Adrienne Rich or the raw self-revelation of an Anne Sexton, Stone's characteristic voice is that of her "Absinthe Granny": wise, sardonic, crafty, and misleadingly simple. Wearing her nursery-rhyme rhythms and tight, shorter lyrics like camouflage, Stone cunningly seduces her reader with conversational cadences, then turns with hard brilliance in the final lines—"Mom's 'kicker,'" as daughter Abigail Stone says—to mock the reader's innocence. Meditating on human frailty, greed, cupidity, and need, Stone deliberately avoids the watchful omniscience that attaches itself to public, "political" poetry. When we think of verse that protests war or social atrocity, we recall Robert Bly's furious Vietnam pieces, or Carolyn Forche's moving indictments of American foreign policy in Latin America. But we don't think of Ruth Stone.

Yet Stone confounds us even in this analysis because her work is at times deeply engaged with the violence of history. Despite the safe aesthetic spaces constructed by her short love lyrics, Stone's poems are stitched in history's web, whose pattern of rage, made visible in at least four of Stone's recent pieces from *Second-Hand Coat*, reminds us that the poetic voice outside history is a fiction. What Stone cannot embrace is the role of poet as detached social legislator, however "unacknowledged," in Shelley's terms. To be sure, the mantle of "poet" has never rested lightly even on the most public of writers such as Robert Frost, whose cagey uneasiness with the title reflects its godlike potential. Emily Dickinson's refusal to reveal herself to "an admiring bog" stands as a paradigm of the female poet who scorns a public role unavailable to her. But these intersections of poet and aesthetic practice are only partially helpful in understanding Ruth Stone's unwillingness to serve as self-anointed "Voice" commenting on history. When she unmasks the "antiwar and human rights poems" as heavy lumps of dullness, Stone mocks not only the production (factory-style, in "writers' colonies" and MFA programs) of poetry but also the reverential self-importance that certain subjects alone are guaranteed to generate—a reverence, moreover, that extends to the poet: "The workers," after all, "have to be heavy, / very heavy" (*S-HC* 49).

In contrast, Ruth Stone shuns the Yeatsian pose of the golden bird who sings from a branch balanced above culture's pageant. She interrogates history from the perspective of a woman trapped within it, implicated in the very transgressions she seeks to identify. To be a "heavy worker" in the "Po-Biz" means exuding a moral superiority that sets you apart from "them"—the military-industrial complex, or a corrupt political system, for example. While Stone's disdain for aggression is scathing, she nonetheless recognizes that the line between "good Us" and "bad Them" is not always easily drawn. When violence erupts in poems such as "Translations," "The Miracle," or "The Latest Hotel Guest Walks over Particles That

Revolve in Seven Other Dimensions Controlling Latticed Space," its turbulent arc connects sex and intimacy, the individual and society, male and female. We are inescapably molded by cruelty, contends Stone; our humanity is, in a sense, guaranteed by it. Even erotic desire is history's violent offspring, conceived in the fissures of a social topography fractured by racism and war.

Stone invites us to consider these connections in "Happiness." This shorter lyric's two halves appear joined, at first glance, by the title only. The first stanza describes the ecstatic couplings of a newlywed pair on leave during World War II; the second, the husband's solitary pleasure at the front as he follows a snowbird over the frozen Russian tundra. Stone unites these potentially sentimental images with the bracing frame of war and loss. The husband's bird quest "burns" only in the speaker's imagination because the letters mailed home that described the bird are long gone. So, too, is the bird itself, whose incongruous snowy form on war's frontier mirrors the words that brought it to life in correspondence latticed by the censor's stamp: both existed in spite of the voids—war, "the shadow of a Russian church," the violated letter. More important, the creature represents the fragile possibility of human life outside history: "You followed it beyond sight of the camp, of the others, / as if for a moment there was a choice" (*S-HC* 46).

But choosing to escape is impossible, as the poem's unsettling first stanza insists, and war becomes the uninvited guest in the lovers' bower. Violence, not passion, makes the bed move "as if we had created a miracle": shock waves from an explosion in Port Chicago wash over their room, as "Several thousand pounds of human flesh / shot like hamburger through the air" (46). This jarring juxtaposition presents an old poetic conceit—*petit mort* mimicking *grand mort, grand* mocking *petit*. But because these deaths are anchored in a specific historical event, the memento mori here is literal, not just literary. Stone reinforces the violation of the body through metaphor: pounds and pounds of "hamburger" meat suggest immoderate appetites and raw flesh, an unspoken and macabre parallel with the commingled fleshly appetites of the lovers.

The terrible tragedy of war at home is further tangled by the revelation that the subsequent "bizarre" funerals for these disintegrated enlisted men are no less strange than "certain facts" about the event: "there were no white males / loading ammunition on that ship" (46). What explodes in the night sky is racism in the military. Neither funereal artistry—the "wax," the "closed caskets"—nor poetic artistry can mend this torn flesh, whose rents expose the bones of hypocrisy in the American body politic. The "happiness" these lovers share is an ironic illusion, an accident of skin pigment that keeps the groom off the exploded ship and saves him for the even whiter snows of the European front. Nestled within the vacuum-seal of the love lyric, the newlyweds are only provisionally guaranteed shelter from the corrosive currents of violence that surround them.

"Happiness" wears its antiwar sentiments with deliberate understatement, drawing conventional conclusions about the frailty of human lives against a backdrop of armed aggression. But the place to begin examining Ruth Stone's "political" voice is in a different poem that blends her signature obsessions about life at the molecular level with what is, for Stone, an uncharacteristically direct evocation of modern military conflicts. In "The Latest Hotel Guest Walks over Particles That Revolve in Seven Other Dimensions Controlling Latticed Space," a guest in a dingy albeit "established" old hotel ponders her room's role as witness to the twentieth century's violent second half:

> Paint disintegrates from a ceiling
> that has surely looked down on the bed beneath it
> during World War Two,
> the Korean War, Vietnam,
> the Cuban crisis, little difficulties
> with the Shah, covert action, and presently,
> projected Star Wars.
>
> (S-HC 40)

The list is gloomy, to say the least. This space lets Stone contrast, by implication, the secluded bed and the conflicts that frame it: the humanizing rituals of sex, passion, and reproduction rehearsed on a bed beneath a "sixty watt bulb" versus the dehumanizing technologies of death looming outside. Room 404, "this home away from home" (40), suits Stone's ruminations: a real "home" can be fantasized as a refuge from external forces, but a room for hire—publicly private, in a sense—offers only temporary sanctuary. Its position is far more fragile and thus more suggestive.

This room, moreover, has held dozens of bodies occupying space in historical time; "In fact," purrs the poem's speaker, it

> probably now contains the escaped molecules,
> radiation photons and particulate particles
> of the hair and skin of all its former guests.

Stone presses modern physics into service here with this deliciously abstract speculation, leading her to conclude that history—a record of violent conflicts occupying particular places in time—can be made palpable by patching together the scattered remains of the room's former occupants, spinning in space:

> It would be a kind of queeze mixture of body fluids
> and polyester fibers which if assembled,
> might be sculptured into an android . . .
>
> (*S-HC* 40)

The curious consequence of yoking time and space—seeing "war" as an essential dimension intersected by matter—is plain: perhaps all these military actions can "materialize," be made visible, recalled through the fragments that once occupied the same meridian in time.

The resulting "android" is both vulnerable and dangerous. Capable of being "programmed to weep and beat its head," it stands in the closet, a synthesized "antihero" whose "feet are bandaged with the lint of old sheets." Shouting "'Which war? . . . How much?'" (40), the android as composite human being dramatizes the way we are all the bandaged victims of war, our emotions chirping mechanically, our feet shuffling off to battles that we are powerless to resist. Our participation is predictable, inevitable—like a law of physics.

But the creature is also armed, with "an obsolete rifle, a bayonet" (40): more ominously, the speaker hears the android

> . . . among her blouses and slacks
> and she knows at this moment it is, at last,
> counting from ten to zero.
>
> (*S-HC* 41)

Is this a reminder that war lurks menacingly in our closets, poised to explode the illusion that space shelters us from time? The android-as-bomb would certainly suggest such a reading; its cozily intimate location hints that although we may find ourselves far from World War II, "covert actions," and blooming clusters of Star Wars warheads, they find their way into our lives. But the android is not war as abstraction but rather the sum of "the rubbish of all the bodies who sweated here" (41). It is both war's image and its victim, the self that spawns violence which takes the self as its object. It is the poem's omniscient narrative voice that identifies the horror about to engulf the female guest; and it is the guest herself whose own "neutrinos" have implicitly contributed to the android sculpture. Stone's monster, the dehumanized sum of human particles revolving in space, stands poised to self-destruct. Like a modern Frankenstein, the android awaits its spectacular rampage "at last"; its final act of violence may paradoxically be its only salvation.

Does Stone mean to suggest that we breed war simply because we are human? Is violent transgressiveness so coded into even the smallest human fragments that nothing can stop its ugly inevitability? "The Latest Hotel Guest" would seem to support that view; it sees us as polluting patrons of a global hotel who leak deadly trails of charged "particles." The poem "Translations" identifies the human malaise with much more selectivity, however. One of Stone's rare prose poems, "Translations" explores the intersections between biologically sexed female bodies and the socially shaped genderings of war. Here Stone argues that war is a fundamental ritual in the cultural construction of masculinity. Its life-denying patterns, however, are practiced on women, who bodies serve as peacetime boot camps, where dehumanizing abuse is normalized. To be sure, the connection between male aggressiveness and female debasement is so basic as to be commonplace; the barracks pinup and the battlefront bayonet are complementary equipment, and we've all heard tales of local police forces using centerfolds for target practice. But these behaviors are too often rationalized—even excused—as the regrettable excesses of men in the line of fire. For Stone, there is no difference between battleground and bedroom; and while this, too, may seem commonplace, Stone's treatment of it is anything but clichéd.

Part of the poem's dramatic power stems from its relentless interrogation of Alexander Mehielovitch Touritzen, the speaker's former lover, the "son of a white Russian owner of a silk stocking factory in Constantinople." Her involvement with Touritzen is brief—a college interlude, an adulterous dalliance offering temporary relief from a husband "whose body [she] hated." She describes Touritzen in spectacularly disappointing terms: gullible, "cautious," "vulgar," an "average lover" (*S-HC* 53), a hapless "innocent lecher" (55). With contrived curiosity, she asks, "have your balls decayed?" (53). Why, then, does she make this rather meager specimen of masculinity the subject of an impassioned rhetorical inquisition and then offer him this final invocation: "May you be forgiven"? Forgive for what? by whom? Having lost contact with Touritzen, the poet wonders whether he even survived the war: "Are you burned to powder? Were you mortarized? / Did you die in a ditch, Mehielovitch? Are you exorcised?" (55). How exactly is Touritzen implicated—and Stone does implicate him, by association—in the murder of a Russian girl by German soldiers, or the radiation-related death of Cana Maeda, or the misattribution of Maeda's translations of Bashō by male publishers? What does he have to do with the starving infant smashed against the Spanish wall by its mother, or the cross-dressing hairdresser with whom the speaker lived, years later?

What indeed. All the men in this poem are vain, vulgar, self-absorbed, arrogant, cavalier, and contemptuous, to one degree or another. They "slip inside" women's bodies as easily as Touritzen, a "pimpled obscene boy," slipped a silk stocking on his hand in mimicry of a woman's leg to "pander" his father's goods—his pimples and pandering translating as pimping and prostitution. These men slide into the female form as expertly as the transvestite might shimmy into his falsies and "sequined evening gowns" (54). They insert themselves into the family tree to ensure their potency (the former husband "told my daughter he was her daddy. It wasn't true" [53]). They rip the body apart, as the Germans did to the Russian girl, nailing her remains up for display. Of course, female impersonation is hardly murder, but what these men share is their ability to use women, to appropriate the feminine. By implication, these violations differ less in kind than degree: murder is made possible when preceded by intellectual erasure, erotic possession, transvestism, lechery. Once the habit of annihilating the female Other has been learned, it can be extended to larger contexts, its scale increased mathematically—even to war.

This connection helps explain why Touritzen's narrated "memories of prostitutes / with big breasts" evoke the same response Stone felt toward a friend's account of the invasion of France, featuring scenes of soldiers plunging from "split open cargo planes," "Statistical losses figured in advance." Both Touritzen's "mattress of / mammary glands"—women as maternal upholstery—and the visions of airborne pregnant cargo planes spilling doomed infants (infantry) from the sky have something in common: they distort and parody the female form. Women's bodies, villages, earth—all "ancient and indigenous" (54)—are violated with equal aplomb, not just by German soldiers but by "thin forgotten dirty-fingered" (55) young men like Touritzen, whose indiscretions take place miles behind the battlefront. Stone wants to know not whether he played a role in the war but which one; in demanding accountability, she prevents him from hiding behind the comparative innocence of his mere "lechery." There is no innocent lechery, as the poem makes clear. Indeed, Stone casts her net of scorn wide—"You are all so boring" (53)—indicting everyone from the heroically misguided chess champ who volunteers for the Spanish Civil War to the husband in his chemistry lab, the Princeton geologist, and the hairdresser picking up English professors.

What precisely is being "translated" in this poem? Perhaps it is the language of the female body, that mute form that has served human history as background, landscape, object, Other. It speaks here with rage and sarcasm, refusing any negotiations or reconciliations that might be interpreted as hope. It condemns an international male cast of soldiers, scientists, husbands, and merchants who plunder the body, imprint it with their unleashed atomic "gamma rays," fix it to a fence, roll in it. But each stanza in the poem also serves as a "translation," an attempt to render the universal language of male aggression in more particular terms. In all of this, Touritzen, his small sins figuring large, serves as synecdoche, transformed from the "fig" of the poet's "pallid college days" (53) into the "plum" of her imagination.

In terms of its form, the poem offers another kind of translation, trading the prosaic for the poetic in the final two stanzas. When Stone's questions finally cease, we sense an impending catharsis, as if Stone has once again found her rhythm after the numbing prose inventories of male transgression that literally resist the lyric voice. Stone's last words are part elegy, part blessing and curse:

> Poor innocent lecher, you believed in sin.
> I see you rising with the angels, thin forgotten dirty-fingered
>   son
> of a silk stocking factory owner in Constantinople,
> may you be exonerated. May you be forgiven.
> May you be a wax taper in paradise,
> Alexander Mehielovitch Touritzen.
>
> (S-HC 55)

The poem reaches closure with an ironic benediction. By scorning an "innocent lecher" who "believed in sin," Stone damns Touritzen's reliance on absolution, which allows him to abdicate responsibility for his transgressions. He can sin with impunity, as long as he has the promise of forgiveness; he need never examine his conscience to determine what in fact qualifies as "sin," as that has already been defined, codified, and assigned relative weight. Thus his mammary "mattress" is but a sin of the flesh—not a particularly grievous violation in a culture where masculinity is built on carnal indulgence. Stone fervently hopes Touritzen finds forgiveness in the heaven of his choice: *she* won't exculpate him. Transformed into the waxy sentinel of a cosmic altar, Touritzen as taper is in fact destined to go up in flames.

"Translations" chronicles male transgression against the female body; "The Miracle" extends its argument to include the mind as well. In this poem, the violation is much more insidious because it is normalized in the female psyche. Women aren't simply conditioned to be victims who have learned the custom of brutality; their erotic response is actually created in its image. "The Miracle" has both nothing and everything to do with war because it seeks to isolate the strands of social aggression that eventually get translated into military contexts. It takes racism as its subject, and with its disturbingly offhand treatment of the KKK, Christianity and faith, sexual initiation, the American South, and the nuclear family, "The Miracle" becomes a sardonic *Birth of a Nation*, filmed in part from the perspective of a five-year-old girl temporarily in the company of southern relatives. Although it begins with Uncle Ivan "down there among the sheets" of the Klan, the poem skirts polemic and instead filters its exposé of racism and hypocrisy through a haze of domestic details: the "chicory in the coffee, / fried apples fried potatoes" (*S-HC* 20) that contextualize a philandering, racist uncle, a neurasthenic aunt, and a young cousin's sexual abuse. The "miracle" to which the title alludes ostensibly means the "miraculous" birth of cousin Audry (made possible through Lydia E. Pinkham's Vegetable Compound!). But the poem's other miraculous event is the "birth" of the narrator's sexualized body and brain, both unwittingly primed to participate in male-designed fantasies that make masochistic transgression the essence of desire.

In the poem's opening lines, the narrator as young child watches, from the safety of her aunt's window, the KKK "out protecting little girls" (20). The statement is deliberately droll because it contrasts the way adults have sexualized the scene with the way the uncomprehending child fails to read its political/sexual component. While the speaker cries for her little brother still in the yard, she should, ironically, be crying for herself, a girl soon to be gendered and sexed in specific ways. Little brothers don't need the Klan's protection, but "little girls" do; more important, the nature of that "protection"—implicitly, from sexual violation—has already begun to shape the child's erotic imagination, a murky mixture of black and white, masculine Otherness and female self:

> . . . an old black man in a horse drawn wagon,
> the reins slack in his hands,
> passed slow—the hot road under the wheels
> whispering dust and I'll get you little girl.
>
> (*S-HC* 20)

Aunt Bess's invitation to "come to the window" (20) and Uncle Ivan's presence down "among the sheets" show us, moreover, that both men and women collaborate to give this scene its meaning as a bridge between the private and the social: the sexual desire about to be born in the child's mind, which she will believe is her most intimate piece of personal identity, is already public property. In this way, Stone's skillful blend of domestic and public details here reproduces the birth of the female erotic. The poem hinges on the narrator's ironic revelation that no black man ever violated her, but her cousin Little Ivan did, despite her disclaimer that "I don't remember what he did." That early violation echoes the KKK, with its image of "sheets falling around us" (21) as young Ivan lures the five-year-old narrator under a bed. Little Ivan, we learn later, is fifteen.

Contrapuntal to this is Aunt Bess's hope that "conception" will cement her failing marriage to Uncle Ivan, the

> ... ghost with a business suit under his sheet,
> his shoes dropping so late,
> coming in whiskey-arrogant, from tarts,
> from parlor chippies, Aunt Bess said.
>
> (*S-HC* 20)

By merging Klan sheets with marriage-bed linen, Stone reinforces the link between social violence and male sexuality, reminding us that the erotic is political, in a sense—socially constructed and irrevocably wedded to a moment in history. The narrator underscores its power by admitting that puberty revitalized the memory of cousin Ivan, already dead and in a pauper's grave seven long years, "killed out west in a stolen car":

> After all that fuss he was my only molester,
> the dark body I was prepared for, the fiery cross
> between my legs. And I began to keep him under my sheets;
> I wore him out in the creases of my brain.
>
> (*S-HC* 21)

Little Ivan slid "under [her] sheets" while everyone's attention was conveniently diverted to the fiction of the dangerous black male outside. Both images cross-pollinate and blossom in the speaker's emerging sexual imagination, where Ivan becomes the emblem and object of the adolescent girl's fantasies. Ivan isn't scary, he's sexy; his violations, rather than short-circuiting her desire, instead define it. Stone invites us to unravel the connections here between race and desire in the American imagination, a knot of violent displacements and denials.

Aunt Bess's situation compounds the uneasiness of Stone's message. Reprobate, womanizing Uncle Ivan fathers the miraculous child, Audry, only provisionally because, as the narrator's mother insists, "Lydia E. Pinkham's Vegetable Compound," which Bess took to get pregnant, "did it . . . little Audry came out of the bottle / of tonic" (21). Audry's conception resembles nothing so much as an ironic virgin birth, for which Bess has coupled with a debased, unholy "ghost" who lurks under publicly and privately sanctioned sheets. Ivan and Bess represent two predictable positions in the social/sexual matrix: the uncle who brandishes his sexual voracity versus the aunt who suffers in victimized silence. But the simple polarities of passionless female and sexualized male are transformed by race—more accurately, by racism. "Whiskey-arrogant" Uncle Ivan flaunts his sexual conquests to Bess, but that self-assurance depends upon his sheet-parade in the streets, where Ivan's sexual primacy is built on the black man's emasculation. The "fiery crosses" become magic erotic talismans that guarantee Ivan's power to protect little girls from sexualized demons of his devising. In contrast, Aunt Bess—headachy, weepy, unwell—uses Lydia Pinkham's tonic to bulwark her body from her husband's violent erotic energy. It becomes her prescription for passive resistance against the dark intruder under *her* sheets. Bess preempts Uncle Ivan's Christian crusade by staging a send-up of the virgin birth: because she succeeds in spite of Uncle Ivan—indeed, without him—Bess emasculates *him*. Not surprisingly, shortly after the birth of Audry, Uncle Ivan "just disappeared" (21).

When Stone embraces Little Ivan, the white cousin has been transformed into the image of the impermissible black male, the only image through which a discourse of sex—albeit a white fantasy of uncontainable black sexuality—can be spoken. The unmistakable power of that imagery waits like a genetic code, imprinted on the child's imagination:

> Purple bodies hung in my head.
> Fiery crosses burned in my bed.
> Aunt Bess talked about this."

(*S-HC* 20)

By making the enemy the black Other, Uncle Ivan—and more generally, white patriarchal culture—hopes women will not discover that the enemy is already between their sheets, threading their dreams, charting the parameters of their desire through currents of hypocrisy, hatred, and violence. Moreover, by perpetuating and enforcing that deception, the Uncle Ivans unwittingly transform themselves—and their sons—into the dark poles of forbidden desire, to be subverted as Aunt Bess subverts Uncle Ivan, or to be embraced furtively by its daughters and nieces for whom desire represents taboo and absence, discovered in the arms of a long-dead cousin. The erotic becomes a simulacrum of sensuality mazed in mental revisitations. Stone reinvokes that lost image in the creases of the text, on the sheets of *Second-Hand Coat*.

"Political" poems are relatively scarce in Ruth Stone's body of work, but not because she lacks interest in history's violent themes. Indeed, Stone cares too deeply about brutality, aggression, and war to talk about them in conventionally self-righteous ways. The verses discussed here represent a distinctly female perspective, yet their earthy engagements with body, sex, sin, and passion are not the work of a pale pacifist: moral outrage need not be squeamishness or self-importance. By localizing, humanizing, and even ironically humorizing her antiwar comments, Stone avoids the lugubrious cement packaging she so dislikes. Most important, however, Stone finds in these verses a reflecting mirror in which we may see ourselves with a double consciousness, as both victims and occasionally unwitting perpetrators of the horror. Even Stone is not above lying to Touritzen the devil; her white skin glistens in the raging fires of Port Chicago, and her erotic desire straddles a chasm of racism. The android in the closet is herself.

14 *Experiencing Otherness*
Ruth Stone's Art of Inference
Roger Gilbert

> If the blower is on
> you may experience otherness—
> > > —Ruth Stone, "When the Furnace Goes
> > > On in a California Tract House"

Ruth Stone has slowly but surely come to be recognized as a major autobiographical poet and is treated in those terms elsewhere in this volume. But in addition to being one of our finest poets of the self—or, to be precise, of her own warmly specific self—Stone has also shown herself to be unusually devoted to otherness in all its varied forms. Other lives, however dimly known, exert a powerful claim on Stone's imagination, and she's developed a wide range of ways to acknowledge that claim without turning the other into a mere projection or image of the self. In this essay I'll be concerned not with Stone's many portrait poems, in which she sketches in the particulars of some forlorn individual like "old Bessie" in "Proce-dure" (perhaps a cousin of Auden's Miss Gee), the Masons in "Sunday," or Mrs. Dubosky in "What Can You Do?," but with those poems in which another person or entity is shown from a distance, as both indisputably real and frustratingly inaccessible. Stone's answer to the challenge posed by such glimmering manifes-tations of otherness is the act of mind commonly known as infer-ence, which might be defined as a marriage between observation and imagination. Where acts of reference posit some direct knowledge of what they present, acts of inference advertise their own lack of solid grounding; beginning with some bit of empirical evidence, they move outward to imagine an unseen yet plausible reality beyond. Inference can never produce certainty, of course, since it always involves an irreducible element of guesswork, but it allows a poet like Ruth Stone to approximate a knowledge of the other without assuming the kind of imaginative hubris necessary to claim full and secure possession of the other's mystery.

The poem that most purely exemplifies Stone's special use of inference is "Second-Hand Coat," which is given pride of place in her volume of the same name.

> I feel
> in her pockets; she wore nice cotton gloves,
> kept a handkerchief box, washed her undies,
> ate at the Holiday Inn, had a basement freezer,
> belonged to a bridge club.
> I think when I wake in the morning
> that I have turned into her.
> She hangs in the hall downstairs,
> a shadow with pulled threads.
> I slip her over my arms, skin of a matron.
> Where are you? I say to myself, to the orphaned body,
> and her coat says,
> Get your purse, have you got your keys?
>
> (*S-HC* 1)

It's possible to read this poem as an allegory of the self, in which the coat symbolizes the acquired crust of "second-hand" values, customs, and habits, while its wearer represents the truer, more skeptical part of the self struggling not to become a mere adjunct of its social garb. Such a reading is certainly consistent with Stone's self-portrayal throughout her work, yet I think it obscures the crucial role of otherness in this poem, not just as a dimension of the self but as a powerful challenge to the moral imagination of the poet. If we read the poem not allegorically but literally, what comes into focus is a gradual process of inference and extrapolation that culminates in a moment of uncanny yet sadly prosaic vocalizing. Stone manages the transition from observation to inference with great tact. As the speaker feels in the coat's pockets, we can easily suppose her to be finding "nice cotton gloves" and other clues to the owner's identity, but at a certain point we realize the process of reconstruction has gone beyond the narrowly deductive and entered the realm of the imaginative. Suddenly the accumulated details fuse into a recognizable human image, a "her" with whom the speaker feels herself merging through the quasi-magical agency of the coat. Through metonymy, the coat itself then takes on the woman's being, metamorphosing grammatically from "it" to "she." This series of transformations reaches its climax as the coat's wearer imbues it with the power of speech and asks it for some word of wisdom, to which the coat can only reply with weary, automatic phrases: "Get your purse, have you got your keys?" In this poem, inference runs up against its limits. While it can summon the absent, perhaps dead woman's image and even give her a kind of life, it cannot make her speak with anything more than the voice of ancient habit.

The desire to make the dead speak is of course a principal obsession in Stone's work. Her autobiographical poetry has for the last thirty years been dominated by the single fact of her widowhood, which inspires many of her most haunting poems. What concerns me here is the way bereavement opens a space in which the other can be apprehended with shocking immediacy. Several of her poems establish a triangular relation among the speaker, her lost or absent lover, and some third party only tangentially linked to the other two who nonetheless takes on great presence and pathos. It's as though the intimacy that had once belonged to the speaker and her lover gets displaced or refracted onto some accidental encounter. Perhaps the best example of this dynamic is the poem "Winter":

> The ten o'clock train to New York,
> coaches like loaves of bread powdered with snow.
> Steam wheezes between the couplings.
> Stripped to plywood, the station's cement standing room
> imitates a Russian novel. It is now that I remember you.
> Your profile becomes the carved handle of a letter knife.
> Your heavy-lidded eyes slip under the seal of my widowhood.
> It is another raw winter. Stray cats are suffering.
> Starlings crowd the edges of chimneys.
> It is a drab misery that urges me to remember you.
> I think about the subjugation of women and horses;
> brutal exposure; weather that forces, that strips.

In our time we met in ornate stations
arching up with nineteenth-century optimism.
I remember you running beside the train waving good-bye.
I can produce a facsimile of you standing
behind a column of polished oak to surprise me.
Am I going toward you or away from you on this train?
Discarded junk of other minds is strewn beside the tracks:
mounds of rusting wire, grotesque pop art of dead motors,
senile warehouses. The train passes a station;
fresh people standing on the platform,
their faces expecting something.
I feel their entire histories ravish me.

(*S-HC* 18)

In the final poem of her book-length sequence *Who Is the Widow's Muse?*, Stone's most sustained exploration of widowhood, the muse admonishes the grieving poet: "'We must get back to the real thing. / The blood and meat of the world'" (*WM* 59). "Winter" beautifully charts the mental process that carries the poet from an engulfing sense of loss "back to the real thing," the immediate realities of other lives. From the outset, memories of the beloved are interwoven with awareness of present things, but at first the speaker only registers other lives with a kind of vague, detached pity that mirrors her deeper self-pity: "Stray cats are suffering," "I think about the subjugation of women and horses." The thought of the beloved is the one insistent, even violent reality here, opening the widow's wound like a letter knife breaking a seal. But as the poem proceeds, the balance of power begins to shift subtly. The turning point comes with the line "Am I going toward you or away from you on this train?" While the remembered moments that the speaker invokes have become progressively sharper, she now recognizes that her trajectory may in fact be away from the past and the lost, toward something strange but real. Even here otherness is defensively, even contemptuously objectified: "Discarded junk of other minds is strewn beside the tracks." But the speaker's attempt to contain and distance the demands of other minds through scornful metonymies like "senile warehouses" can't be maintained, and in the poem's closing lines she turns herself fully toward "the blood and meat of the world":

> The train passes a station;
> fresh people standing on the platform,
> their faces expecting something.
> I feel their entire histories ravish me.

The hint of sexual violence in the word "ravish" suggests that these "fresh people," with their unknowably complicated histories, have moved into the space formerly occupied by the remembered lover and have even taken on something of his importunate power. To apprehend these people not just as props for a scene of mourning and memory but as individuals with their own private histories of loss and gain requires enormous negative capability on the speaker's part. As the poem ends, we know nothing of these people—they haven't been described or individuated in even the most cursory way—yet the fact of their presence has been acknowledged with moving honesty, as it had not been before.

Another poem, "Icons from Indianapolis," traces a slightly different entanglement between erotic memory and violent otherness. Here the remembered lover is not the dead husband but a youthful boyfriend named Mike Tarpey ("Once when he kissed me I swooned" [*S-HC* 37]), who keeps the speaker waiting downtown for hours, and sometimes never comes for their assignations at all. The speaker's long vigils again create a space within which to view the other:

> I could see the older black woman in the bus station,
> pus running down her legs, gushing out of her,
> the policeman coming to take her away. What were hats
> and fur shawls when I knew that? She never left me.
> From that time I carried her like an icon.
> In these catacombs also he lies in perfect condition;
> age nineteen, black hair, his thin jaw slightly out of line.
> Was it that Picasso-like shift in planes that I could never
> look at enough? These go with me where I go.
> I wrap them in linens without prayers. I carry them.
>
> (*S-HC* 37)

After the tenderly nostalgic evocation of Mike Tarpey that begins the poem, the obtrusion of the black woman and her obscure yet horrifying plight seems wholly unexpected. What's most striking is the absolutely equivalent status the poet grants to the nameless black woman and the named lover: both are "icons from Indianapolis," sacred objects to be faithfully preserved in memory. Where "Winter" follows a movement from lover to other, this poem establishes a kind of equilibrium between the intimate and the strange, refusing to choose or privilege one at the expense of its complement. The Picasso-like beauty of the young man and the pathos and terror of the old woman (vaguely linked to diseased sexuality) are equally central to the poet's image of Indianapolis, and so equally to be cherished.

At times in Stone's work, otherness is manifested more obliquely than by direct visual encounter. A number of her poems show the speaker meeting dim traces of another person and finding them all too insinuating; a poem from *Cheap* called "Room" is an example:

> Someone in the next apartment
> Walks slowly back to a room abutting mine.
> I am on this side, sitting.
> It is uncomfortable trying to be quiet.
> For weeks coming in here to change my clothes,
> I think, are my clothes too daring?
> And the sound of water rushing in
> Filling a tub in the other room
> Makes a loud continuity,
> As though many people might be living here,
> Twining their arms about me,
> Passing me in the hall,
> Making tender jokes.
> Sunlight enters the room near the ceiling.
> And shadows of leaves letting go
> Flash in downward slants
> Falling inside the room
> To sink through the floor.
> And I think
> Is this the way it will be?
> And I listen
> With my ear against the plaster.

$$(C\ 26)$$

Here the contrast between the speaker's total lack of concrete information and the inferred presence of the other becomes almost comic. The speaker's anxious sense of the other's impingement on the privacy of her room is partly undermined at the end of the poem, as she stands with her ear against the wall, hungry for knowledge of her neighbor. Clearly she is ambivalent about the life beyond the room, which seems potentially both loving and strangling: "As though many people might be living here, / Twining their arms about me." The shadows of leaves falling inside the room prefigure some more ominous invasion: "Is this the way it will be?" But the promise of continuity, "tender jokes," the warmth of human presence, keeps the poem from becoming an exercise in paranoia. The unseen, muffled but undeniable otherness beyond the wall is both threat and charm, calling the speaker to exercise her powers of inference despite all her self-protective instincts.

Otherness in Stone's poetry does not invariably assume human form. Many of her poems focus on inanimate objects endowed by the poet with sentience and personality. These poems are predominantly playful in tone, yet it would be a mistake to view them merely as anthropomorphic jeux d'esprit. What makes the speaking objects in Stone's poetry more compelling than the animated clocks and teapots in a Disney cartoon is their essentially moral claim on the poet, which is finally hard to distinguish from that of the black woman in Indianapolis or the people in the train station. "Comments of the Mild" may serve as illustration:

> The cabinet squats trembling on its carved legs,
> an essence of trappings. Inside on the awkward shelves,
> a cast-off bedspread, two stolen books.
> From no period at all; in fact, the back legs are not carved,
> while the front ones have turned balls. It tries to be Spanish,
> Louis Quinze, Sheraton, Hilton Plaza. It is a bastard
> from a tract house. There was no cabinetmaker.
> It grew with a lot who were cut on band saws,
> glued together on an assembly line, and stained
> in a warehouse. "I am furniture," it says, in a subdued voice.
> Not useful, not even ornamental, it has a certain bulk
>   presence.
> It takes the place of those who are not with you.
> When you wake in the night, you sense that you are not
>   alone.
> There is someone else. But you forget who it is.
> Sometimes passing the cabinet, you open the part that looks

like the confessional box. It is stern and empty.
Nothing fits in there, not even your head.

(S-HC 33)

The poem's title offers a hint as to the source of this decidedly
ordinary cabinet's strange authority: it serves as an instance of
"the mild," a category that encompasses human as well as inhuman
beings and which is commonly linked to "the meek," exalted under
Christianity. With its awkward construction, its confused motley
of styles, the cabinet struggles vainly to take on some minimal
dignity but fails, "a bastard / from a tract house" and not a product
of artisanship. The only identity it can claim is the most generic
one: "'I am furniture,' it says, in a subdued voice." This subdued
voice is not unlike the voice of the second-hand coat, unable to do
more than rehearse old habits. And yet this wholly nondescript
object nevertheless becomes a *presence* as the poem progresses ("it
has a certain bulk presence"), one that asks to be recognized. "It
takes the place of those who are not with you": once more the
absence of the beloved provides an occasion for the other to make
itself known. Like Frost's woodpile, the cabinet exudes a ghostly
sense of selfhood: "When you wake in the night, you sense that
you are not alone. / There is someone else. But you forget who it
is." Its very homeliness or mildness seems to invite inference as a
more impressive object might not, suggesting a history of band
saws and assembly lines, appealing to the poet with all the pathos
of the perennially overlooked. In a final irony, however, she reminds
us that this object resists even the kind of negative capability that
allowed Keats to enter a billiard ball: "Nothing fits in there, not
even your head." Subdued, stubborn, recalcitrant, the cabinet
squats, asking to be known but refusing to divulge itself, its "confessional box . . . stern and empty."

If otherness can be found within the room as well as without, it
may also appear in the realm of the body itself. Several of Stone's
poems meditate on parts of the human anatomy, imagining them
as independent beings with their own concerns and quirks, as in
"Message from Your Toes":

Even in the absence of light
there is light. Even in the least electron

there are photons.
So in a larger sense you must consider your own toes.

The poem begins with the familiar pattern of absence giving way to presence, this time at the subatomic level, then veers into an Alice-like discussion of the speaker's toes and their assorted messages. Rather than leading the speaker's mind away from the pain of loss, however, her toes offer their own gentle lament:

> And your toes, passengers of the extreme
> clustered on your dough-white body,
> say how they miss his feet, the thin elegance of his ankles.
>
> (*S-HC* 25)

Deep calls unto deep, and toe reaches for toe: Stone infers for her feet a desire specific to their nature. Touchingly funny as this poem is, it represents another version of the impulse to give voice to the other that runs throughout Stone's work. A poem like this demonstrates that the other may reside not on the far side of a wall or even in a corner of the room but on the very margin of the body.

As the first three lines of "Message from Your Toes" suggest, Stone has a long-standing fascination with the submicroscopic realms of molecules and atoms. One reason, we may surmise, is that they offer a way of estranging the familiar, of discovering otherness within the most intimate regions of the self. As she writes at the opening of "Moving Right Along":

> At the molecular level,
> in another dimension,
> oy, are you different!

The poem proceeds to unfold a bizarre phantasmagoria in which the body's particles host a Republican rally while the self stockpiles "rancid vitamins" that in turn become

> . . . farmers
> marching to Washington,
> . . . helpless to stop
> the grinding laws of entropy.
>
> (*S-HC* 10)

The humor in this strange tale of subatomic politics reflects Stone's playful intuition that even in these invisible zones, some drama of

force and counterforce can be inferred. A more serious attempt to
locate political meanings "at the molecular level" comes in the poem
"The Latest Hotel Guest Walks over Particles That Revolve in Seven
Other Dimensions Controlling Latticed Space," which presents
an extraordinary apocalyptic vision of history, bodies, and atomic
debris. Once again we're inside a room mysteriously permeated by
otherness: "Tiny flakes of paint glitter / between the hairs on her
arms." The paint disintegrating from the ceiling of this dismal hotel
room speaks of a larger history of destruction; the poet reminds
us that the same ceiling has

> . . . looked down on the bed beneath it
> during World War Two,
> the Korean War, Vietnam,
> the Cuban crisis, little difficulties
> with the Shah . . . and presently,
> projected Star Wars.

At this point the poem's focus shifts from the panoramic to the
minute:

> In fact, within that time,
> this home away from home, room 404,
> probably now contains the escaped molecules,
> radiation photons and particulate particles
> of the hair and skin of all its former guests.
>
> (S-HC 40)

An eerie, almost palpable sense of the room's lived history starts
to emerge, reminding us of the second-hand coat, the faces in the
station, the clumsy cabinet, all of which resonate with their own
past. The invisible vestiges of the room's former occupants offer
nothing to the senses yet still serve as invitations to inference,
spurring the poet to give a face and voice to these vanished others.

When she does so, however, it's with a dramatic twist that propels
the poem from the inferential to the visionary:

> It would be a kind of queeze mixture of body fluids
> and polyester fibers which if assembled,
> might be sculptured into an android,
> even programmed to weep and beat its head
> and shout, "Which war? . . . How much?"
> She feels its presence in the dim artificial light.

It is standing in the closet.
There is an obsolete rifle, a bayonet.
It is an antihero composed of all the lost neutrinos.
Its feet are bandaged with the lint of old sheets.
It is the rubbish of all the bodies who sweated here.
She hears it among her blouses and slacks
and she knows at this moment it is, at last,
counting from ten to zero.

                                        (*S-HC* 40–41)

This astonishing trope is worthy of the great M. R. James, who also conjured up strange beings from the residue of empty rooms. Unlike the owner of the second-hand coat, this creature transcends particularity; it is a kind of collective demon, haunted by the endless repetitions of historical trauma. But it remains also a mere inference: "She feels its presence in the dim artificial light." In this poem Stone carries the inferential impulse beyond the otherness of single histories and aims it at the otherness of history itself. The poem's central insight is that no particle is an island, just as no room can be insulated from the "blood and meat of the world." The terror of nuclear holocaust invoked by the android's final countdown only confirms the mutual implication of selves and others; all perish as one when the final zero sounds.

Through all these investigations of otherness, Ruth Stone keeps her sense of balance intact. Neither detached nor bullying, her poetics of inference yields up a provisional knowledge of others without losing sight of their ultimate opacity. Whether the other is a person in a station or in the next room or in the past, or even a chunk of inorganic matter, Stone feels its being as a kind of insistent demand for recognition. While her point of departure is always resolutely empirical—a glimpsed face, a sound, a bit of debris—she allows herself to probe tentatively into the psychological and metaphysical regions that these data imply, reminding us over and over that what we see and what we can't see but know is there are of a piece. Hers is not so much the stone Dr. Johnson kicked to prove the physical reality of things as it is the fabled philosopher's stone, whose mere presence enables revelations to occur.

15 *The Clever Widow*

Grief-Work, Humor, and Narrative in Ruth Stone's Poetry
Janet Lowery

In 1989, Ruth Stone accepted a teaching position at SUNY at Binghamton for the spring semester, and as a dutiful graduate student in the creative writing program there, I found her book *Second-Hand Coat: Poems New and Selected* on a bookshelf in our library, pulled it down, absently flipped it open to "Codicil" from *Cheap*, and read:

> I am still bitter about the last place we stayed.
> The bed was really too small for both of us.
> In the same rooming house
> Walls were lined with filing cases,
> Drawers of birds' eggs packed in cotton.
> The landlady described them.
> As widow of the ornithologist,
> Actually he was a postal clerk,
> She was proprietor of the remains.
> Had accompanied him on his holidays
> Collecting eggs. Yes,
> He would send her up the tree
> And when she faltered he would shout,
> "Put it in your mouth. Put it in your mouth."
> It was nasty, she said,
> Closing a drawer with her knee.
> Faintly blue, freckled, mauve, taupe,
> Chalk white eggs.
> As we turned the second flight of stairs
> Toward a mattress unfit for two,

Her voice would echo up the well,
Something about an electric kettle
At the foot of our bed.
Eggs, eggs, eggs in secret muted shapes in my head;
Hundreds of unborn wizened eggs.
I think about them when I think of you.

                                        (*S-HC* 58)

I reread the poem several times, immediately engaged. That marvelous first line directly admits to bitter feelings but is curiously devoid of spite, a smart technique that takes the sting out of the line and brings us closer to the poem via piqued curiosity. The odd near-absence of an overt blaming tone indicates the speaker's sense of perspective while providing relief from tension produced by the word "bitter." A note of finality is struck with the phrase "the last place we stayed," yet the wide-open quality of the line's tone carries a whisper of humor, an undercurrent of light irony that ripples through the poem.

The second line gives us the cause of bitterness—a too-small bed—and it is such a trivial cause, so indirectly connected with the addressee himself and so much more associated with place and situation that the disappointing bed becomes a detail of endearment. Again anxiety is reduced, interest piqued; the size of a mattress is not expected to cause bitterness, yet one can identify with the pettiness. The poem moves on to the walls lined with filing cases, those "Drawers of birds' eggs packed in cotton," and it mentions the landlady for the first time, the ornithologist/postal clerk's widow, who climbed trees to collect eggs for her husband and put them in her mouth to keep from falling down or dropping an egg; the landlady whose knee shoved a drawer shut in a detail sharply familiar for anyone who has done housework. The cleanly physical image of the knee and the snappy tone embedded in the line transfer a straightforward quality to the landlady's performance of household duties and convey a matter-of-fact attentiveness to the speaker in her observation of that performance. By including one specific report of a domestic act by the landlady, Ruth Stone opens a window into the rarely acknowledged world of women watching other women go about the tasks relegated to women, a source of interest, albeit unwitting or unwilling interest, to many of us. We are curious about how other women decorate and maintain their homes, how they keep up with housework, and what their attitudes are toward domestic tasks. The details about the landlady and the rooming house provide some of this important information, and through incidentals such as stacked filing cases lined with cotton bedding for birds' eggs and the reference to the kettle at the foot of the bed, we get the picture of a woman who maintains her establishment in shipshape order yet remains eccentric in her methods of keeping the memory of her deceased husband. The focus on the landlady's odd shrine to her dead husband links her to the widowed speaker, who memorializes her husband through poetry.

"Codicil" flashes back in time to refocus the lens of memory and adjust it to the death of the addressee, and in the process it re-sees the past. All the descriptive particulars of the rooming house—the electric kettle, the filing cases, the flight of stairs, and those "Faintly blue, freckled, mauve, taupe, / Chalk white eggs"—carry the poignancy of a memory retrieving details of the past in an effort to sort through them. The catalog of eggshell colors is so deftly presented that they appear in *our* heads in some sort of multiple array of "Eggs, eggs, eggs in secret muted shapes," and then the poem ends in the brilliant understatement, "I think about them when I think of you." That final line moves us as readers to understand the connections between the speaker's identity as widow and the associations she makes in the poem's imagery: wombs packed with unfertilized eggs, the dead husbands' wizened scrotums, and the spooky, hindsighted link between the poem's speaker and the character the poem focuses on for roughly fourteen of twenty-six lines: her sister in the otherworldly realm of widowhood, the landlady. "Codicil," like so many of Ruth Stone's poems that look at the subject of loss, exemplifies a brilliant consciousness working on the monumental task of grief.

If loss is a primary subject of poetry, then a combination of remembrance and grief is its work, and who has taken that task more seriously than Ruth Stone? Her poetry bears witness to various stages of grief-work in poems written with a controlled, self-reflexive humor that reveals anguish spiced with wit and acceptance.

Stone's poetry of remembrance does not bog down under the excessive weight of self-importance or self-centeredness. Often buoyant, always powerful in its poignancy, her poetry on grief is an act of generosity, a study in resilient devotion, a tour through the underworld of loss that so many of us dare not enter. In poems such as "Codicil," Stone charts a course through the particular griefs of the widow in language that blurs the line between shades of sorrow and shades of humorous self-awareness. Laugh and weep, she seems to say, and then weep and laugh. She gives us her human example in the human exercise of grief, and her poems model how to grieve without sinking into despair. But it is the fresh imagery delivered in a direct tone of voice that convinces me of her brilliance. In "Loss," also from *Cheap,* she writes:

> I hid sometimes in the closet among my own clothes.
> It was no use. The pain would wake me
> Or like a needle it would stitch its way into my dreams.
>
> (*S-HC* 59)

These lines inspire awe and envy because that needle stitching into dreams is a perfect icon for grief moving on its sharp, slender path through the soft dimensions of consciousness, an image that could come only to a writer of rigorous honesty at a dear price. In "Turn Your Eyes Away" from *Second-Hand Coat*, she writes,

> The gendarme came
> to tell me you had hung yourself
> on the door of a rented room
> like an overcoat
> like a bathrobe hung from a hook . . .
>
> (*S-HC* 47)

In these lines, the direct delivery practically knocks one over with the power of a figure that evokes so much because it is startlingly familiar in multiple ways. The likening of the dead body to a coat or robe hanging on the door of a room is instantly visible in its slack form. The body hangs as if a familiar garment, but it is a shell, a corpse, devoid of life, as is a coat or robe. In addition, the extra detail of the hook on the door echoes the physical configuration of someone hanging by the neck with eerie accuracy and hints at the connotation of a "hook" as an exiting prop. And then the stunning lines: "when they forced the door open / your feet pushed against the floor" (*S-HC* 47). Since the feet can represent various aspects of sensuality and are linked to the heart in the language of symbols, the focus on them is grimly tender because the feet of a loved one are so cherished, so intimate. In "Years Later," also from *Second-Hand Coat*, the language eventually works its way down to the feet:

> Through hexagonal holes, sections
> of your arms appear, or the fingers
> of your right hand, our innocent obsessions,
> your eyebrows, individual hair follicles,
> or the Mongol pockets of fat
> along your high arrogant cheeks.
> These parts of you are clear
> and reasonable and finally tell me
> that it is your skeleton I crave;
> the way the bones of your feet,
> fitted like the wing sockets of angels,
> came toward me in time over the long
> plateaus of ice; their delicate mouselike tread
> printed in tracks of snow over my mind.
>
> (*S-HC* 42)

These lines are so oddly serene that they terrify. Tying a sense of longing with images of skeletal afterlife, linking an icy, ethereal mental realm with notions of romantic destiny in maddeningly intelligent language, the imaginative leaps executed here are not to be underestimated, nor is their impact. The poem transports us to a wilderness in the tundra of a mind searching for connections to the lost "other" through the "bones of the feet," "the Mongol pockets of fat," the "high arrogant cheeks," and other "innocent obsessions" of happy conjugal relations. Examining the boundaries of time, the dimensions of love inside the workings of the heart, the poem explores a scary realm, desolate and remote. Yet the profound familiarity of this inner territory suggests that grief is not the frontier from which we must distract ourselves; it is the land we inhabit without awareness. However irrational it may sound to say

> These parts of you are clear
> and reasonable and finally tell me
> that it is your skeleton I crave

the use of the word "reasonable" establishes the rationality of the expression. We crave the physical embodiment of our longing, we crave the physical dimension, the physical reality from which our senses draw their sustenance; we crave the symbols of what was once familiar, what we once believed we possessed. In poem 14 from *Who Is the Widow's Muse?* (which has numbers rather than titles for most of the poems), the use of imagery related to the feet again asserts its significance in the iconography of romantic love:

> Even her stockings, even her shoes,
> wept for him.
> Her shoes in their pockets
> noticed he no longer
> knocked them aside.
> He is dead, they dreamed,
> what is the use of the bows on our toes?
> The widow thought,
> "Were hints of the muse hidden here?
> Could the muse be fetish?
> Could it be footwear?"
>
> (*WM* 16)

The childlike tone behind the shoes' need to question the most flirtatious, feminine frill on their tips belies a simultaneous sophistication in the nature of the question. What need femininity its decorative symbols without the masculine to impress? asks the poem, in a question that achingly evokes the loneliness of the widow's existence. Sad with humor, the poems in *Who Is the Widow's Muse?* are packed with rueful observations, ironies, and intimacies projected on the page in small, explosive expressions of a feminine mind counting her losses, mining her experience to outwit grief in a veritable riot of "gender and sorrow" (*WM* 15). Both mythical in proportion and refreshingly down to earth, Stone's poems give figure to a process and render, in language rare and rarified, human comprehension of the infinite and the intimate.

Stone once remarked in passing that she wondered if her poems would be taken more seriously if they were less humorous. Although the subject of loss is often associated with her work, particularly her more recent collections, perhaps her sly wit has persuaded some readers and critics that her poetry kids around too much and is therefore not worth a great deal of serious commentary. In "Being a Woman" from *Cheap*, she wryly makes a note on what my mother calls "talking to the wall":

> You can talk to yourself all you want to.
> After all, you were the only one who ever heard
> What you were saying.
>
> (*S-HC* 75)

However, it is precisely her keen wit that softens the edge in the subject matter of her poems and displays the intelligence propelling them forward. Never shrill or forced in tone, her poems zing with the speed of a quick mind; they sing with humor and poignant reflection.

Although her poems frequently read like icons of awareness, small jewels that capture and preserve moments of consciousness, they can also read like extremely compressed narratives complete with character, setting, dialogue, and plot. Poem 47 of *Who Is the Widow's Muse?* asks, "does a story exist like a chair? / Is a bed a story without words?" (*WM* 53). When asked by Robert Bradley in his chapter in this volume to "distinguish between what might be considered a narrative poem and a lyric poem," Ruth responds that "most poems are narrative, no matter what you say. I don't think you can name a poem that doesn't have drama at its center." Because Ruth Stone writes poems that can be described as both lyric *and* narrative, both image-laden *and* drama-centered, her work is difficult to appreciate without disregarding the lines of demarcation drawn in critical debates positioning narrative in opposition to lyric. The sense of narrative in her work does not clash with its image orientation, and, frankly, positioning narrative in poetry *against* the conventions of lyric in poetry is a contrivance. All poems seek resolution in language, and Ruth Stone writes poems that draw on both narrative and lyrical conventions.

Take "Translations," for example, a brilliant, lengthy apostrophe from *Second-Hand Coat* addressed by a female speaker to "Alexander Mehielovitch Touritzen," the "son of a white Russian owner of a silk stocking factory in Constantinople" (*S-HC* 53). An essentially narrative poem, it opens with a quick-paced catalog of memories about a former lover and musings about his fate, only to explode into a complex web of anecdotes, observations, and accusations regarding male/female interactions that seeks to distinguish between crimes and misdemeanors. One of the most engaging aspects of this poem is the speaker's unabashed account of sexual game-playing with a man obviously obsessed with his own sexual exploits. "Forty-five years ago," she states in the opening lines,

> . . . we rumpled your rooming house bed
> sneaked past your landlady and turned your plaster Madonna
> to the wall . . .

Structured like a braid of stories related to the speaker's romantic adventures and her dry observations about men, the poem is propelled by questions pumped at the absent Touritzen, inlaid with internal slant or full rhymes and coy confessions of the speaker's manipulations and infidelities:

> . . . Are you out there short vulgar civil-engineer?
> Did you know I left you for a Princeton geologist who called
>   me
> *girlie*? Ten years later he was still in the midwest when he
>   died
> under a rock fall. I told you I was pregnant. You gave me
>   money
> for the abortion. I lied to you. I needed clothes to go out
>   with
> the geologist. You called me *Kouschka*, little cat. Sometimes I
>   stopped by the civil-engineering library where you sat with
>   other
> foreign students. You were embarrassed; my husband might
>   catch you . . .
>
> > (*S-HC* 53)

The poem turns the tables on more common literary scenarios, in which male narrators report on exploitive sexual activities with women or complain about unfaithful lovers, to give us, instead, a rollicking account of a woman able to work the male characters' weaknesses in her favor and then tell her side of the story without a sense of shame tainting the delivery. It's tit-for-tat in the world of the flirtatious, brainy, and presumably attractive female speaker of "Translations," a female speaker who does not alienate women readers because she is not braggadocios or vain or hampered by guilt regarding her fun with men; gleefully she offers up her experiences with the opposite sex as an example of "the way it is," or at least "the way it was."

The underlying and very subtly intoned lesson being given by the poem is not a warning for women to beware of philandering men, or vice versa, nor does it caution women or men to refrain from sexual exploits; it is a far more serious look at deeper signs of male vanity, destructiveness, and misogyny, and it speaks to all readers. The male world takes some hits in this poem, but, again, the poet's direct tone avoids blame, sticks to examples of violence that offend or victimize women, and declines to arrange a litany of whines or complaints against male sexual behavior. Placing flawed human sexual behavior in perspective against examples of organized atrocities committed in Nazi death camps, the poem weighs sin against sin, compares the death from exposure to radiation of a female Japanese scholar and other tragedies of war to sexual obsessions, sexual infidelities.

"Translations" gives us a clever female speaker who takes advantage of men in the bedroom, so we are not forced to listen to another woman's bitterness toward men in that arena; rather, we hear a female voice documenting male foolishness about matters of sex: "my husband the chemist . . . came back in the flesh fifteen years ago. . . . / He told my daughter he was her daddy. It wasn't true." These lines are followed by a slippery little sentence that is unobtrusively tucked between two important anecdotal passages: "You are all so boring" (53). Slipped in as it is without qualification, the line forces the reader to look at how it was set up in the poem and from there draw conclusions. The absent-for-years-husband is made to look like a cuckolded fool for claiming paternity of the speaker's daughter. Apparently, it is men's claims or concerns about virility that bore the speaker, and perhaps that is why the poem frolics so through the speaker's escapades with men.

Later on in the poem, the following lines about Touritzen—

> Those afternoons in bed listening to your memories of
>   prostitutes
> with big breasts, how you wanted to roll on a mattress of
> mammary glands . . .
>
>   (*S-HC* 54)

—convey a picture of a giant infant man rolling around on fleshy female body parts, but the image is silly, not romantic or appealing. He is described in various stanzas of the poem as an "Average lover" (53), a "Pimpled obscene boy" (54), and is addressed once as "Old fetid fisheyes." Grotesque rather than sexy as a character, Touritzen is referred to as a "Poor innocent lecher, [who] believed in sin" (55). If "innocent lecher" seems like a contradiction to some, it is not in the logic of the poem, for the point of the piece is to suggest that sexual activity of the sort described in the text—between two consenting adults—is innocent behavior when compared to the actions of those responsible for

> . . . The ripped-open
> remnants of a Russian girl nailed up by the Germans outside
>   her
> village. . . .
>
>   (*S-HC* 54)

That Alexander Mehielovitch Touritzen "believed in sin" is made quaint by the tone of this line, but the poem hints that his belief is also a blessing of sorts, a type of innocence in light of the atrocities of war and their inherent disregard for moral law. In the poem's last stanza, the speaker asks that Touritzen be forgiven his petty sexual transgressions, exonerated for his small-time offenses, that he live on as "a wax taper in paradise" (55). There is an irony at work here that keeps the poem buoyant despite its serious underpinnings, but again, to the speaker of the poem, Touritzen's sexual sins are so lightweight and easily forgiven that they deserve celebration in the afterlife when compared to the sins of violent aggressors against humanity.

Although "Translations" has strong narrative elements, the language is so packed with detail, rich in imagery, and fluid in movement that it has the newfangled quirky, speed-demon textural quality of postmodern lyric poetry. We see "plaster Madonnas" (53), "sequined evening gowns," "cracked bones," "kimonos . . . burned on the flesh of women in the gamma rays of Hiroshima," "silk stockings," "foam-rubber falsies," "slime paths of microorganisms," and Touritzen's "sainted mother's soft-dough body: her flour dusted breasts" (54). The poem swells and drops and careens around corners on a roller-coaster ride of image-decorated anecdotes that keeps us visually and aurally stimulated as it weaves its patterns of observation, criticism, and exoneration. Narrative in structure, sly in strategy, the poem presents a complex problem and seeks its resolution, as do lyrical poems. What is the problem? It is the question of how to weigh lesser evils against greater evils, or distinguish minor transgressions from those that seem unforgivable. Finally, the poem means to import knowledge through a sense of experience and indicates it from the very first words: "Forty-five years ago." The invocation of age implies wisdom and asks us to listen up; thus the poem commands attention. It does not, however, hit us over the head with an embarrassing naive, humanistic self-righteous attitude, and it does not speak from a position of self-importance. The tone, as usual with Ruth Stone, stays light, and the poem closes with humorous internal and end rhymes, plus a few glorious yet funny blessings on the head of Alexander Mehielovitch Touritzen. Dramatic and lyrical, narrative and imagistic, smart with sound and richly musical, the poem has sweep, it has depth, it has intelligence. It is one of the most important poems written in English in the postwar period, and yet I have not found it in any anthology that includes postmodern American poetry.

Having written fantastic, musical, entertaining, and intelligent poems for forty-five years, Ruth Stone is perhaps just now reaching her peak as a writer. "That Winter" is a brilliant example of some of her most recent work. Set in Chicago during the war, it manages to touch on various forms of racism and violence, both stateside and abroad, both domestic and war-related, perpetrated by females as well as males, all of it rolling from the speaker's tongue like a quaint story about the time period that ends with the lines

> You know by now there
> isn't much to live for
> except to spite Hitler—
> the war is so lurid
> that everything else is dull.

> (*Sim* 10)

The sensitivity and awareness, the wry compassionate stance expressed in the poetry of Ruth Stone confronts, amuses, comforts, and entertains. Pointing to the human condition, the human experience, her work explodes the boundaries of awareness; it opens up the world and examines the terrible beauty of its innards with an unflinching perspective. Using a shorthand of leaps, her quickest of minds produces poems that are never sluggish or ponderous in movement; rather they make quick high-IQ leaps of consciousness. If tone comes from perspective and perspective is derived from distance, angle, attitude, and various perceptual screens, then tone can reveal infinite nuances of personality, and in Ruth Stone's work, the intelligence and warmth of personality is so particularly engaging that it often startles me with a type of rare and irresistible clarity. The light and lithe quality of the musculature of her poems, even when their subject cuts into serious matters, conveys a sense of mental agility, an impeccable ear, a warm proximity to subject matter, a wisdom of the body that knows what it knows through the senses and the cells of the skin. Capable of connecting the laws of physics with the Song of Songs, Ruth Stone is a poet of loss, a poet of great wit, a poet of breathtaking lyrical imagery and sophisticated narratives. A brilliant writer, a genius with language, she is a poet to be celebrated, anthologized, and carefully studied.

16 "Who Is the Widow's Muse?"

A Memoir and Reading of Ruth Stone
Aliki Barnstone

My first memory of Ruth Stone is also one of my earliest child
hood memories. We were walking barefoot in the small stream
beside her house in Vermont. I stopped to look at a flower or a
rock, and when I emerged from my reverie, Ruth was gone. I was
frightened and called, "Ruth! Ruth!" and walked through the dark
conduit under the road. The conduit's spooky metal ribs closed in
on me, a child's underworld where we kids often ventured in play.
Then I walked into sunlight and found Ruth digging in her garden,
peacefully distracted. It's said that the factual accuracy of childhood
memories are not as important as how they are remembered. It's
also said that people who die and come back from death report the
sensation of tranversing a dark tunnel toward a bright light. My
memory intuits a crucial theme in Ruth's life and poetry: her quest
into the underworld to reunite with Walter, her husband who died
in 1959. In this process, she resembles the mythological figures
Psyche and Orpheus, who for love crossed into the land of the
dead. She makes the journey through morbidity into resurrection
repeatedly. It is a form of poetic practice as seen in "Habit":

> Every day I dig you up
> And wipe off the rime
> And look at you.
> You are my joke,
> My poem.

Your eyelids pull back from their sockets.
Your mouth mildews in scallops.
Worm filaments sprout from the pockets
Of your good suit.
I hold your sleeves in my arms;
Your waist drops a little putrid flesh.
I show you my old shy breasts.

(*C* 15)

In this poem, as in my memory, Ruth is a gardener. Like all
gardeners, she nurtures the blooms with the rotting dead. As a
poet, she is a gardener of corpses, fertilizing with the dead man
who was her husband. But this concentration on death turns on
itself and becomes life-giving, a way of raising him from the dead.
The poem is morbid, but not merely morbid: it portrays a recurrent
fantasy, a habit of mind. The pun in the title refers both to frequent—perhaps automatic—behavior and to clothing. Because her
devotion is to a dead man, the desire to reunite with the loved one
means taking on the habit of a nun, the clothing of death. Yet this
act, this remembering, is also an act of creation (a "poem"), is
humorous (a "joke"), and at the end is sexual and tender ("I show
you my old shy breasts"). The language of the poem moves in and
out of symbolic patterning ("You are my joke, / My poem") to the
detailed and rooted in reality ("Your eyelids pull back from their
sockets"). This movement from the concrete to the abstract, from
"putrid flesh" to the translation into poetry, tells her joke: the harsh,
grotesque reality of death is also the substance and subject of her
poetic production. As Ruth asks in *Who Is the Widow's Muse?*,

Is the muse the inexorable
law of death?
Is my claim to the muse
no more than my own breath?

(*WM* 14)

Out of morbidity comes what is needed to sustain the psyche:
poetry, humor, erotic love. For Ruth Stone, poetry is survival; and
her life and work are through necessity concerned with survival.

Ruth was born in 1915 in Roanoke, Virginia, and grew up in
Indianapolis. She was raised in the rhythm of music and poetry.

Her father was a drummer and her mother read the poems of Tennyson to her, she tells us, from the time that "she started suckling me at her breasts."[1] Her grandmother set up an easel in her kitchen. In this familial community of artists, she began writing at the age of seven. The poems were, Ruth remembers, "a physical rush coming through. And then the poem would write itself. . . . the thing knew itself already. I didn't know it. . . . And I can remember running into the house, blindly groping for pencil and paper."

She married Walter Stone, a professor and critic, and with her three daughters led the life of poet and faculty wife until 1959, when their happy marriage ended tragically with Walter's suicide in Cambridge, England. She returned to the United States where she took a job as an editor at Wesleyan University Press. After a year, she decided to move to her house in Goshen, Vermont. She began teaching at universities, moving from one year-long appointment to another and returning to Vermont for vacations and dry spells.

During the summers, my family lived about twenty minutes away from Ruth's place. When we visited, we would all cook a large spaghetti supper, sit around the fireplace, and talk, and everyone, children and adults, played the Poetry Game, in which we went around the room, each saying a word, then, using those words for inspiration, wrote poems and read them aloud to each other. The only way to lose was not to write a poem. No one ever lost. Her home, like the home she grew up in, is a place where artists are cultivated. Ruth says, "All children are poets and the parent who loves the poetry is the one who preserves the poet. It's the parent who isn't perceptive who kills it. Otherwise, we'd all be singing birds." I grew up in a similar home—my father is a poet and my mother is a painter—and my parents preserved the artist in us, just as Ruth preserves the artist in her daughters and in all, child or adult, who are lucky enough to know her.

Those nights in Goshen—outside was the cool night and the wonderful darkness, unlit by any city—let the lights of a vast Milky Way shine in the smell of hay and woodsmoke. Inside, I felt charged by poetry and by our circle. The sense that the poem is "a physical rush" that "writes itself" develops, I think, out of a freedom that the child-self feels when those around her or him delight in imagination. Not only were we appreciated, but we appreciated the writing of our friends and family. I was charged with the electricity not only of my own lines, but with the anticipation of hearing the poems of others. As a child I learned from experience that hearing and reading poetry inspires poetry, that carrying the poems of others inside helps me to hear the tune of my own poetry.

Ruth's enthusiasm for the work of family and close friends extends to students. She is a wonderful teacher. Wendy Barker calls her a "guardian angel" who "tells the truth," who "takes your poems as if accepting a valuable gift" and "reacts to those truths so far down you're amazed she sees, she knows" (325). When she taught at Indiana University in Bloomington, where I grew up, I sat in on her workshop, held at the house she rented in the country. Though the conversation was the adult conversation of writing students, the atmosphere that Ruth created of delight in the art transported me back to Goshen.

Ruth says she "obsessed," that her writing is "except for my emotional commitment—the most important thing in the world to me." She writes everywhere, all the time. Once "I'd decided I just simply had to write this story. . . . I put my foot on the door and the children were on the other side beating on the door. And I wrote that whole story with my foot on the door." As a child, I remember we ran an errand in her battered blue station wagon. We parked in front of the farmhouse and she wrote a poem on a paper bag. I sat in the passenger seat, listening to the engine click in the afternoon heat, watching her pause occasionally to rest her head on the steering wheel and think, then watching the large, looping strokes of her handwriting appear on the brown scrap of paper. I suppose this moment was my model when I wrote a poem on an old envelope in a traffic jam in San Francisco, waiting to get on the Bay Bridge!

While she is obsessed with her own writing and is the parent, teacher, preserver, and guardian angel of other poets, she has been published often through the efforts of others. Walter sent her poems out to magazines and sent her first book, *In an Iridescent Time*, to Harcourt Brace. When it was rejected, he sent a letter back saying,

"How *dare* you not publish this book?" It was published the year of his death. Later, it was through Bill Goodman, her editor at Harcourt Brace, that *Topography* and *Cheap* were published. Ruth's book *Second-Hand Coat* came out with David Godine, when Goodman worked there. But in the years 1973 through 1986 she published no books because Goodman was at Harvard, where they publish no poetry. When Sandra Gilbert asked her why she didn't send out her work, she replied, "I don't know. It's so much trouble. I guess I really forget. Honest to God, I forget. I have poems mixed in with bills, letters, junk, and when I was really sick a few years ago I thought, why don't I do what Walter used to do?"

While this information may seem to paint a portrait of dependence, it may be more useful to think of it in opposite terms. She says, "A part of me has been totally isolated and independent all my life and that's my writing. And I've never depended on anyone about that—nor ever taken a course or ever asked anyone." As Gilbert notes, Ruth has not played "the game of 'Po Biz.'" And comparing her to Emily Dickinson, Gilbert admonishes us to "remember Ruth and others like her, women who make their art in obscurity and discomfort" (324). This obscurity and discomfort is paradoxically both imposed and chosen, a kind of obstinance. Ruth says her writing is "so private. I can understand Emily Dickinson. When I began getting published . . . you won't believe this—it was in my second marriage, with Walter, who was a brilliant man and normally ambitious both for himself and for me. And through him I learned about ambition and recognition and all of those things." She protects her gift by focusing on the art, not on the recognition. Dickinson, in her famous poem "I'm Nobody! Who are you?" writes:

> How dreary—to be—Somebody!
> How public—like a frog—
> To tell one's name—the livelong June—
> To an admiring Bog!
>
> (288)

Similarly, Ruth sees the dreariness and the cost of being "somebody." She says, "If you're playing power games and if you're fascinated by that sort of thing, it takes up all of your mind. It takes up all of your imagination." Ruth's poem "Wavering" echoes Dickinson's "I'm Nobody," though Dickinson's poem is satirical and lighter and Ruth's, while satirical and characteristically humorous, is heavy, devastating in tone:

> What makes you think you're so different?
> That was my weaker self hanging around outside the door.
> The voices over the telephone were accusing, too.
> "Must you always be you?" (They had the advantage,
> More bold without faces. They swirled a few icecubes
> With a suggestive pause.) For a moment
> I took my heart out and held it in my hands.
> Then I put it back. This is how it is in a competitive world.
> But, I will not eat my own heart. I will not.
>
> (*C* 89)

That Ruth, as Gilbert puts it, "hesitates to put herself forward" (324) may be a way of keeping that independent part of herself independent. She does not resist being put forward by others; she does resist promoting herself and the consequence of self-promotion, which is suffering internal "wavering." "This is how it is in a competitive world": the messages from that public world ask her to compromise herself, to give in that "weaker self" who would relinquish her imagination, her "difference," in order to conform. Those accusatory voices who have the advantage, complacent with cocktails on ice, can with their demeaning "Must you always be you?" drive the self to take out its heart, that is, to extinguish acting, feeling, or writing from the heart. The cost is a spiritual, if not a physical, death, because the authentic self, the one that is always itself, is silenced. So, at the end, Ruth is emphatic: "But, I will not eat my own heart. I will not."

Ruth's knowledge of her own independence and vision—her steadfast self-reliance—combines with a sense of helplessness not only before the fact of suffering, and of death, but before the power of her own creativity: "the poem would write itself. . . . And I can remember . . . blindly groping for pencil and paper." These themes come together in a crucial poem, "The Plan." which I hear often in my mind's ear:

I said to myself, do you have a plan?
And the answer was always, no, I have no plan.
Then I would say to myself, you must think of one.
But what happened went on, chaotic with necessary pain.
During the winter the dogs dug moles from their runs
And rolled them blind on the frozen road.
Then the crossbills left at the equinox.
All this time I tried to think of a plan,
Something to bring the points together.
I saw that we move in a circle
But I was wordless in the field.
The smell of green steamed, everything shoved,
But I folded my hands and sat on the rocks.
Here I am, I said, with my eyes.
When they have fallen like marbles from their sockets,
What will become of this? And then I remembered
That there were young moles in my mind's eye,
Whose pink bellies shaded to mauve plush,
Whose little dead snouts sparkled with crystals of frost;
And it came to me, the blind will be leading the blind.

(*TOP* 33)

"But what happened went on, chaotic with necessary pain." Life dealt her cruel blows, yet she goes on determined not to "eat" her "own heart." There is a deep despair in this poem, yet it is coupled with a curious acceptance. There is no sense in which a plan will "bring the points together," but there is her powerful ordering imagination in the face of the incomprehensible and disorderly. The woman speaking in the poem, blind as she is to her fate, has the power of vision: "Here I am, I said, with my eyes." Her mind's eye transforms the moles "Whose little dead snouts sparkled with crystals of frost" into the revelation at the end of the poem (though it is a kind of antirevelation, since it sees its own blindness): "And it came to me, the blind will be leading the blind." Everyone, even—or perhaps especially—the animals, is both implicated and embraced in this statement. Both dogs and moles, oppressors and oppressed, act out of blind instinct. For all of us, what happens does so "chaotic with necessary pain." There is a wry edge, a dark humor in the use of the cliché at the end of the poem. There is also a tenderness, a way in which the points, or at least people, do come together in their attempts, stumbling through the dark though they are, to lead anyone anywhere.

Not to have a plan is a way of being. Ruth says, "It seems as though I'm always facing something that I don't understand. I seem to have to take things in through my pores." A plan does not intervene, filtering out vision. As in so many poems, death is internalized in "The Plan." The moles on the "frozen road" are not only observed but transplanted to the "mind's eye." There is an immediacy. Everything, even the past, is in the present tense because the past, taking its place in the mind's eye, lives in the self. Planlessness is a form of love, an openness, a submission to memory, as in "Osmosis":

> If I decide it is better to be me than you
> I will need to discount that your hair is thick and long,
> At the same time knowing that some who are not yet born
> Will die early and pitiful. Out of blue eyes
> Bluer than any strange gray blue I have ever seen
> You look back at me, your bluejeans the same
> Faded cloth everywhere walking away from me.
> I am torn out of myself thinking it is better
> To be this moment aching that I am
> Also being you remembering me now.
>
> (*C* 91)

As in "The Plan," the speaker internalizes what is other than oneself; "it is better" than discounting the excruciatingly beautiful—and present—details: the texture of the hair, the blue of the eyes. The poem dislocates the boundaries of the self and of time; it questions the notions that self or time can be *located* at all. The most common article of clothing—blue jeans— has the power to bring back the past, to make the present always the past, to evoke the absent loved one: all blue jeans are "the same" as the ones worn by her or him. Likewise, the loved one who is still present ("looking back" or "walking away") is also past because she or he is already committed to memory by the speaker. The ubiquity of blue jeans reminds the speaker of the human burden of death, that the young—for blue jeans are associated with the young—are mortal, and that youth is transient; so the speaker perceives "the same / Faded cloth

everywhere walking away from me." In the last three lines, the
categories of time and self merge into each other:

> I am torn out of myself thinking it is better
> To be this moment aching that I am
> Also being you remembering me now.

The "I" is at once the "you" and is the present moment itself. And
the "I" is also the past where the "you," by remembering the "me
now" into the present, becomes the speaker. So the speaker, "I,"
becomes the "you" recreating the "I." Ruth is always recreating
herself through the eyes, feelings, and desires of her creations. It
is her way of sharing the worlds of her loved ones in order to find
herself.

Because the processes of osmosis and separation relate to the
maternal, and because the images of long hair and blue jeans relate
to youth, "Osmosis" feels to me like a poem written to one of
Ruth's daughters. Yet the poem's epistemology is the one Ruth
developed out her widowhood and, of course, out of the particulari-
ties of self that preceded Walter. Walter's suicide intensified and
transformed Ruth's vision, as can be seen in her poetry's characteristics of a terrible and tactile loss, returning to the loved one through
memory, and the fluidity and boundarilessness of time and self.
Ruth's *Who Is the Widow's Muse?* is a sad, wonderfully funny, and
profound exploration of the title's question, which is never directly
answered in the book, though each section of it proposes an answer.
The muse is sometimes "he," sometimes "she," sometimes "it." Is
the muse "simply fat" (*WM* 8), "a key" (25), "effervescent" (41), or
the widow's "dead mother" (12)? Perhaps the widow's muse "resides
in the bladder" (20), "has an omnivorous appetite" (4), is "fetish"
or "footwear" (16), "a marble statue / . . . painfully shattered" (31),
is "envious" (37), "carnal," or has "hot pants" (33). All these possibilities, and more, are entertained. And we readers are entertained by
the widow writing poem after poem and letting us peek in on her
process as she calls on the muse again and again ("'I'm worn out,'"
the muse says in one of her feminine semblances; "'Don't abuse
me'" [*WM* 38]). Only one thing is "law": time is released from

the limits of chronology. The widow, like Billy Pilgrim in Kurt
Vonnegut's *Slaughterhouse Five*, is "unstuck in time":

> "Everything will disappear,"
> she thinks.
> There is no past.
> Even the widow's muse
> is subject to these laws.

> (*WM* 30)

Though "Everything will disappear," what disappears, as in "Osmosis," becomes present in the rememberer and in her transformation
of the past in poetry: "There is no past." The drama of writing poetry
in *Widow's Muse* is a triangular one in which the widow and her muse
and the dead husband interact. In the proem of *Widow's Muse*, "All
Time Is Past Time," Ruth sets forward her fluid poetics in which time
and self without boundaries combine to create "the word":

> Goliath is struck by the stone.
> The stone turns into a bird.
> The bird sings in her window.
> Time is absurd. It flows backward.
> It is married to the word.
>
> This is the window of the giant's eyes.
> This is the bird singing alone.
> This is the river of forgetting.
> This is the chosen stone.
> This is Goliath's widow.
>
> Struck by the stone he leaps
> into the future. He lies
> a monolith, a rune, light
> from a distant nova. Not even a bone
> remembers begetting him ever.
>
> The song is a monotone.
> She is the word and the window.
> She is the stone and the bird.
> She is the bed of the river.

> (*WM* prologue)

Just as in Wallace Stevens's "Domination of Black," in which
each entity—the leaves, the wind, the flames, the fire, the tails of

the peacocks, and the hemlock—"turns" into every other entity, so in Ruth's poem, Goliath, the stone, the bird, the window, time, the word, the river, the widow, and so on, all turn into each other. Also like Stevens's "Domination of Black"—which Robert Hass has written was the first poem that made him "swoon"—"All Time Is Past Time" creates a swoony feeling, as if reading it, one found oneself in a vortex of the river. Because of the poem's circularity, it is difficult to know where to begin to speak about it. Yet this circularity is an openness, an inclusiveness, that invites the readers in, connects with them, and asks them to imagine further associations.

"All Time Is Past Time" bears an affinity with T. S. Eliot's opening lines of "Burnt Norton," the first of "The Four Quartets":

> Time present and time past
> Are both perhaps present in time future,
> And time future contained in time past.
>
> (213)

Yet Ruth's poem is more personal, concrete, and engaging because she makes emotionally tangible why time collapses in on itself. Through his death, Goliath's widow becomes his eyes, his window on the world, his voice, and his singing bird. She is everything that he was alive; when he dies, "he leaps / into the future" of her memory. Death creates osmosis, a horrible oneness for the married couple, yet simultaneously creates ultimate separation and loss. So the widow is also "the bird singing alone," singing her elegy, a solitary woman and writer. He and she "flow backward," in "absurd time," in "the river of forgetting," for even as he lives in her memory, he is lost, forgotten. Nothing can be known without forgetting. A person cannot be remembered wholly, only in fragments, perhaps like the fragments the poet has spun into the vortex of the poem.

The widow is both the word and married to the word. She is all time; she is "the bed of the river," the river of time, the bed of marriage and making love, the bed on which the river "flows backward" into the arms of a living Goliath, into forgetting, and the deathbed. Her marriage to the word, though, is fraught with guilt and hostility. For if she is the stone, she is the stone that killed

Goliath. David, who threw the stone that killed Goliath, is also the singer in the Bible; many of the psalms are attributed to him. The widow is the one left behind, who transforms the loved one into words. She chooses the words and the "chosen stone." In her memory and words he is a Goliath, a biblical figure, larger than life, rather than a man. The widow feels implicated in her husband's death, so she is the stone, the Ruth Stone, that struck Goliath. Yet she also blames him. He is the "monolith," the "chosen stone," that struck the giant dead. He is the stone, Walter Stone, and he chose his own death, and perhaps the widow's. For she is everything he is, and he is dead.

The risks of remembering are great, for the process of osmosis described in the poems above means being "torn out" of oneself, suffering endlessly from guilt, and anger, and conflict. Over and over the poems speak of being broken, of being pulled out of oneself, of a death inside. In "Mine," a dream poem, she writes that "sick at heart" she lies down "among those who dream of murder":

> I have died ahead of my body.
> It drags behind me.
> Come, they say, hiding their smiles,
> Surely you can do something
> About this bloody thing that is following you.
> You know it is yours.
>
> (*C* 61)

On the one hand, the poem is about a desire to dispose of one's own body. It is a dream of suicide. On the other hand, taken in the context of her other poems, I cannot help but think that the "bloody thing that is following" her is Walter. The pattern of absolute union coupled with absolute separation, seen in "Osmosis," "All Time Is Past Time," and so many other poems, recurs here and in "Becoming You," which begins:

> I think about territory
> And how you invaded my skin.
> Now I shall grow
> Until I encompass you.
>
> (*C* 14)

The consequence of Walter's traumatic death is that the "territory" of separate selves has been abolished: he "invades" her; she
"encompasses" him. The sexual implication and power of those
verbs is important. In a sense, this unclear territory of selves is the
issue everyone must contend with in intimacy, but the violence of
invasion and encompassing is, in this case, the language of the
special state created when one of the people in a couple has died.
There is no other to mediate, so everything must take place within
the one left alive. The memory of the other person becomes a
disease: in "Becoming You" the disease invades her skin; in "Mine"
she is sick at heart. For her, his body died ahead of him; in "Mine,"
she dies ahead of her body. The cure, at least in this poem, is a
dream of double murder. If she kills herself, she kills him, too,
balancing the scales, putting them both in the same realm. This
tormented balancing act is portrayed in terms of justice in "Denouement":

> You intimidated me. I was thrown into hell without a trial.
> Guilty by default. It was clear the murdered one was dead.
> There were only two of us. But no one came to lead me
> away.
> A hundred eyes looked in and saw me on fire.
> We loved him, they said. Then they forgot.
> After many years I knew who it was who had died.
> Murderer, I whispered, you tricked me.
>
> *(TOP* 17)

This poem is the flip side of "Osmosis" and of *Who Is the Widow's
Muse?* in which there is an acceptance and even a celebration of the
fluid boundaries between the territories of selves: "it is better" to
remember. But in "Denouement" is rage and bitterness over the
legacy of suicide. A suicide demands remembrance. It haunts and
points an accusing finger at the survivors, especially the closest
survivors. As wife, Ruth is "intimidated," "thrown into hell without
a trial. / Guilty by default." Not only does she accuse and intimidate
herself, she feels "A hundred eyes" of others doing the same. The
poem seeks to demolish the tautology "It was clear the murdered
one was dead." This is the pivotal line of the poem, characteristically
humorous at the most devastating moment. Only she knows he is

not completely dead. Though she does not say it explicitly, she is unlike those who say they "loved him," then "forgot." She did not forget, and not forgetting, died. The "murderer" at the end of the poem, like the body that the accusers at the end of "Mine" say is hers, is more ambiguous. The murderer has murdered himself or her or both. The "trick" is that who was murdered by whom is never "clear."

The language of the poem is duplicitous, a riddle. And it is a fitting language, for this kind of riddle is "hell" for her because it means being guilty eternally and having no authority to "lead" her "away." This intense feeling of being left alone, with no accepted truths for solace, recalls "The Plan" and the absence in that poem of "Something to bring the points together." The "trick" for Ruth is the transformation of these questions into poetry, another kind of legacy that involves the issue of forgetting and refusing to forget. Ruth's poetry is her legacy, not Walter's, no matter how present he is in it. Her poetic power leads to another kind of guilt because there is a sense in which Ruth usurped Walter's life and death and made it one of the primary subjects of her poetry.

I prefer to see from the perspective of resurrection, however. The price of resurrection, poetic practice, and love is guilt, feeling broken, invaded, tormented, and sometimes dead. It is part of the bargain Ruth has struck with the world—and "Bargain" is the first poem in *Cheap*:

> I was not ready for this world
> Nor will I ever be.
> But came an infant periled
> By my mother sea,
> And crying piteously.
>
> Before my father's sword,
> His heavy voice of thunder,
> His cloud hung fiery eyes,
> I ran, a living blunder.
>
> After the hawker's cries,
> Desiring to be shared
> I hid among the flies.

Myself became the fruit and vendor.
I began to sing.
Mocking the caged birds
I made my offering.

"Sweet cream and curds . . .
Who will have me,
Who will have me?"
And close upon my words,
"I will," said poverty.

(C 3)

The poem is both a complaint and a proclamation of herself as poet. Through intimidation and hard luck, oppression and poverty, she has shaped herself into a poet, "into fruit and vendor," and by singing her verse she wins her freedom, "Mocking the caged birds." Yet the cost of her freedom is her desire thwarted. She wants to be noticed, to be "shared," not as "a living blunder," but as the free bird who sings despite the patriarch's thunder. She has become luscious, but poverty takes her. Though unlike Ruth, Emily Dickinson did not have to contend with real economic poverty, she did face a poverty of intimacy and society. And, like Ruth, Dickinson used "poverty" as a metaphor for her loneliness and for her unfulfilled desire. Dickinson saw this kind of poverty not as hardship but as "beauty" because it "enlightens":

Want—
Enlightening so well—
I know not which, Desire, or Grant—
Be wholly beautiful—

(801)

Similarly, Ruth allows herself to be embraced by an absence. She transforms her loneliness and her desire to be shared into her poetry. Through her poetry, she attempts to make the word the flesh that she so dearly misses. Ruth recalls, "Fifteen years, sixteen years, we lay—we lay every night of our lives together, wrapped in each other's arms. We really loved each other. We were really—he thought we were twins." Though words are bodiless, a poet can hear poverty say, "I will," like a marriage vow. Through poetry Ruth sees

> . . . you . . . coming toward me,
> We are balanced like dancers in memory,
> I feel your coat, I smell your clothes,
> Your tobacco; you almost touch me.
>
> (*TOP* 13)

In these pages I have concentrated on death in the love poems. I hope this focus will be seen as one of many possible starting places in an exploration of the body of Ruth's work, a part of the whole, not the whole. In "Bargain," Ruth is not only a widow but a woman surviving alone in the world, confronting not only the metaphorical poverty of loneliness but an absence of money. One thing I learn from Ruth's poetry is that the world must be seen with compassion and humor, no matter how bitter the losses; that we are all alone together and deserve attention and particularity. When Ruth writes, "I smell your clothes, / Your tobacco; you almost touch me," her words are tactile. The significance that she gives to the particular carries over to poems on other subjects. And her subjects are many. There are wonderful poems to her daughters, to friends, to neighbors, to vegetables, poems about places, traveling on buses, nature poems, poems explicitly feminist, poems whose subjects defy categorization. She is a survivor, and her poems give full resonance to the word. In her poems, people and things survive in the splendor of the quotidian.

The last poem of *Who Is the Widow's Muse?* reads:

> The widow is told by a great seer
> that fifty-two is a magic number.
> She consults the muse.
> "We must get into a higher gear,"
> the muse whispers. "We must shift
> out of this phase."
> "Just one more about shoes,"
> the widow begs.
> The muse shakes her head.
> "No. We must get back to the real thing.
> The blood and meat of the world."
> The muse took the widow in her arms.

"Now say it with me," the muse said.
"Once and for all . . . he is forever dead."

(*WM* 59)

But it doesn't matter that he is "forever dead." "All Time Is Past
Time." So Walter, forever dead though he may be, is always present,
dead and alive. The poem may be cathartic, but it is not the final
catharsis. It is poem number fifty-two, "a magic number" to end a
book. Just as Walt Whitman, that most cyclical of poets, chose to
end his "Song of Myself" with the fifty-second section, so too
did Ruth Stone. Fifty-two is magic because it makes the end a
beginning—since there are fifty-two weeks in a year—and returns
the reader back to the first section of the book. The insistence of
the muse that the poet repeat the line, "Once and for all . . . he is
forever dead," belies the doubt that Ruth will ever "shift / out of
this phase." The internal debate will continue. Walter, like Goliath,
"leaps into the future." There will be many more poems returning
to him. He will almost touch Ruth. And through her words, he—
and she—touch us. There will be "one more about shoes."

Note

1. All quotations of Ruth Stone's speech come from her interview with
Sandra M. Gilbert, chapter 7 of this volume.

Works Cited

Barker, Wendy. Untitled in "On Ruth Stone." *Iowa Review* 12 (1981): 325.
Dickinson, Emily. *The Poems of Emily Dickinson*. Ed. Thomas H. Johnson.
   3 vols. Cambridge: Harvard UP, 1951, 1955. Cited in text by number.
Eliot, T. S. *Collected Poems 1909–1935*. New York: Harcourt, 1936.
Gilbert, Sandra. Untitled in "On Ruth Stone." *Iowa Review* 12 (1981): 323–25.

17 "Under the Seal of My Widowhood"
Kandace Brill Lombart

But love transcends despair.

—Ruth Stone, "Last Lullaby"

In *Who Is the Widow's Muse?*, Ruth Stone evokes most of the mythological and historical allusions to the widow created by male writers, who have been obsessed with the motif, while women writers have largely ignored it. But Stone incorporates her experience as a widow as well as a wife and mother; and ultimately, from this specific "female vision through a female idiom" (Friedman 966), she introduces her reader to the multiplicity of a female poet's voice by her autobiographical inscription.

Celeste Schenck, in her article "All of a Piece," argues that the process of writing "poetic autobiographies" "is a deliberate strategy" of women poets (292). Specifically, in relation to the widow's reality, Ruth Stone, who tends to use the first person singular "I" throughout her poetry, reflects with lucid sharpness on her life's events. Clarifying and identifying her own space within the widowed "I," Stone emphasizes far more than the singular voice of one widow's experience. Yet, although the poet herself confirms the autobiographical elements in her work, the modern notion of subjectivity in lyric poetry remains an issue for debate. Nevertheless, most of her poems betray a narrator who is also the poet rather than a fictional persona constructed by her.

In poem after poem from *Who Is the Widow's Muse?*, that narrator tackles the "widow question"—that is, all of the mythical allusions and sociocultural impositions a widow inherits with the word. She includes not only the mythological but also the historical allusions to the widow. In the opening poem, the act of suttee is invoked:

> Crow, are you the widow's muse?
> You wear the weeds.
> Her answer, a caw.
> Her black beads:
> two jet eyes.
> A stick fire
> and a thorn for her body.
> Into the wind, her black shawl.
>
> (*WM* 1)

From the outset, Stone refers to all of the major symbols associated with "widow": "weeds," "stick fire," "thorn," and "black shawl." But "A stick fire" also invokes an instant association with one of the earliest literary widows: Dido in Virgil's *Aeneid*.

In the opening lines of Book IV, the widowed Queen Dido's distress is identified as lovesickness for Aeneas ("But now for some while the queen had been growing / more grievously love-sick" [81]). And then Dido reveals to Anna, her confidante, that she is weakened by the complex, contradictory emotions of loyalty to her first husband's claim to her love and the awakening of "the old flame" for Aeneas. "I would rather the earth should open and swallow me . . . ," she says, "before I violate or deny pure widowhood's claim upon me" (81–82). She never remarries, of course, but at the moment Aeneas sails out to sea, she thrusts herself on his sword,[1] then completes her suicide by climbing onto the "lofty pyre" (100).

"Weeds" and "black shawl," quoted in Stone's opening poem, symbolize a widow's mourning and are also associated with Tamar, the first biblical widow: "Then she rose," the biblical text reads, "and left him, and taking off her veil she put on her widow's weeds" (*Jerusalem Bible* 44).

Stone refers to a widow's "shawl" in only two poems in this collection: the one quoted above and "The Widow's Song" ("As my skirt lifted up as a veil, / so the shawl of a widow" [23]). This appears to be a pivotal poem for two reasons: it is one of only two poems given a title (see the prologue "All Time Is Past Time"), and it indicates the woman's transformation from one life stage to another, from wife to widow. No other poem in *Who Is the Widow's Muse?* so nobly, so lyrically evokes the metamorphosis of a woman's life and highlights the celebration of feminine multiplicity. I quote the poem in its entirety:

> As I was a springbok,
> I am a leper.
> As my skirt lifted up as a veil,
> so the shawl of a widow.
> As the oxlip,
> so the buffalo grass.
> As the wall of a garden in winter,
> so was I, hidden.
> As the game of the keeper . . .
> not counted.
> So I am without number,
> As the yellow star grass.
>
> (*WM* 23)

We sense a transformation that dramatizes two stages of a female identity—the states of ripe virgin and sexually discarded widow. In order to move through the poem, the reader needs to make a decision on the use of "as." If "as" functions as an adverb of time, then either "when" or "once" may be substituted. "(Once) I was a springbok / (Now) I am a leper"; I, who sing for all widows, in Hélène Cixous's words, the "self-seeking song" of my widowhood (345). I was once a beautiful gazelle: now I am ugly, leprous, and left alone without a mate. Covered once with the bridal veil of a wife, now I am draped with the "shawl of a widow." Grammatically, "as" or "so" is often used to indicate an exact or close parallel. ("As the game of the keeper . . . / not counted. / So I am without number, / As the yellow star grass.") If "as" is read within this grammatical context, then do we read these lines as an effacement of all widows, left uncounted, abundant as the ordinary prairie grasses that cover the plains? Or, do we interpret the lines as a celebratory declaration of the multiplicity of women? In a dozen brief lines, this timeless "I"—a widow who sings for all widows,—

even Goliath's widow ("All Time Is Past Time")—chants, "So I am without number." The line implies a reference, perhaps, not only to the multiplicity of women but also to the numerous facets of the individual self.

The widow's unveiling is her celebration, her sudden awareness that she is grouped with "all the women of the world" (*WM* 22), who are as common as the first flowers of spring (oxlips/primroses) yet who multiply in numbers in the quest of universal self-identity: "Who am I?" "So I am . . ."

The question still remains, however, "Who is the widow's muse?" In the first poem of the volume, Stone asks, "Crow, are you the widow's muse?" It is clear that Stone's crow is a female entity, clothed in the garments of mourning ("You wear the weeds. / Her answer, a caw"). Rather than a malevolent creature, it appears as a beneficent presence based on Scandinavian mythology. In that mythology, Odin is portrayed as being accompanied by two crows: "Odin/Woden has two ravens on his shoulder, one, Hugin, 'thought' and the other, Munin, 'memory', who ranged everywhere and reported back all they had seen" (Cooper 138).

The widow begins her journey with a muse in the form of a crow/raven or a muse split between "thought" (Hugin), which represents the imagination of the poet and which flies toward the future, and "memory" (Mnemosyne, the goddess of memory and mother of the Muses), which invokes the past.

Stone's crow, unlike the crow from Ted Hughes's violent fantasy world in *Crow*, is a female spirit which is either in flight, or resting, watching, waiting. The only similarities between the two poets' compositions are the rapid timeframe in which the books were composed and the mutual themes of a quest that resolve mourning. Both works also resonate with "mythic motifs." Hughes writes, "Crow's whole quest aims to locate and release his own creator." But Hughes also "alludes to the incompleteness of Crow's quest" (Scigaj 127), whereas Stone completes her muse's quest in a domestically tamed and maternal landscape. The world of the widow and her muse is grounded in the reality of concrete activities (caring for the young children, going to poetry festivals, slipping in and out of shoes, hanging the laundry, dreaming while driving): "I must be serious, the widow thinks, / I must face reality" (*WM* 21). Above all, she encounters the reality of permanent separation from her spouse, emphasized by the muse's admonishment "'We must get back to the real thing. / The blood and meat of the world'" (*WM* 59). In a poignantly maternal gesture, the muse consoles the widow, enveloping her in a nurturing embrace: "'Now say it with me. . . . / Once and for all . . . he is forever dead.'"

Is Walter B. Stone, the poet's husband, her muse—that inspirational force that compels all poets to write? In *Inspiring Women: Reimagining the Muse*, Mary DeShazer posits a fundamental difference between the male and female poet in relation to their respective muses:

Despite occasional attempts to make the muse male . . . no woman poet has imagined a sustained masculine figure comparable to the traditional female muse. Does the woman poet, then, have a muse? If so, what are its sex and nature, and how does it differ from the "inspiring anima" of the male poet?

(3)

To answer the above questions requires an exploration of a potential male muse who appears in the form of Stone's husband in earlier poems. Before determining the identity of Stone's muse in her work, it is necessary to retrace earlier poems in which the widowed, autobiographical "I" of the poet meditates on his eternal absence ("Am I going toward you or away from you on this train?" [*S-HC* 18]). In her poem "Winter," Ruth Stone evokes the "drab misery" of despair, one of the many emotions a widow encounters in her journey of mourning. Yet the nagging memory of him haunts the traveler:

> . . . It is now that I remember you.
> Your profile becomes the carved handle of a letter knife.
> Your heavy-lidded eyes slip under the seal of my widowhood.
>
> . . . .
> It is a drab misery that urges me to remember you.
> I think about the subjugation of women and horses;
>
> . . . .
> I remember you running beside the train waving good-bye.

I can produce a facsimile of you standing
behind a column of polished oak to surprise me.
Am I going toward you or away from you on this train?

(*S-HC* 18)

We are in a space of "raw winter" in New York City. Misery
and debris surround the narrator, but it is most of all the act of
remembering that we are discovering with the poet. "I remember
you running beside the train waving good-bye."

How does the widow escape from the imaginary travel companion who haunts her, watches her, lifts up her "sealed" status of
widowhood, that unbearable wound of loss, which only memory
can slit apart? The letter knife unseals envelopes that conceal
words—perhaps words that are ultimately embedded in her poetry.

The spouse's memory subjugates the widow in another poem in
which the apparition of a male muse is transformed into a "joke."
I quote the entire poem "Habit" in which the love relationship
takes on another dimension with an allusion to a necrophilic desire
to unearth the lover:

Every day I dig you up
And wipe off the rime
And look at you.
You are my joke,
My poem.
Your eyelids pull back from their sockets.
Your mouth mildews in scallops.
Worm filaments sprout from the pockets
Of your good suit.
I hold your sleeves in my arms;
Your waist drops a little putrid flesh.
I show you my old shy breasts.

(*S-HC* 63)

In this daily performance, a "habit" of the poetic imagination, a
grieving woman wipes away the hoarfrost from the leftover body
(note the playful pun on "rime" and poetic "rhyme") to peer at
her "joke," her "poem," and acknowledges the buried lover as an
ironically amusing inspiration for her art. In a seductive gesture,
she offers to expose her "old shy breasts" to the decomposed rem-
nants. The regular act of looking, loving, and metaphorically wish-

ing to "couple" with the muse begets the poem. Thus, in her early poems of mourning, Stone reverses the traditional male poet/female muse paradigm and creates a female poet/male muse relationship.

The autobiographical "I" of the widow and the "you" of the spouse in the two poems cited above pose a question about the muse's identity. Can the muse be interpreted as her dead spouse? It's interesting to note that many of her poems over a thirty-two-year time span (from the moment of Walter Stone's death in 1959 to the publication of *Who Is the Widow's Muse?* in 1991) refer to a male muse; but even the poet herself questions the paradigm:

> Is he the muse?
> The fire irons
> remind the widow of his grave.
> Down or up?
> The devil smiles benevolently.
> "We all love him" he says,
> ashes falling from his teeth.
>
> (*WM* 6)

Are there any precedents for the doubleness of the husband/muse in both love and death? A misreading of a masculine presence in the guise of a devilish muse ("Is he the muse? . . . / The devil smiles benevolently") in Stone's quest cannot be altogether dismissed within the context of nineteenth-century paradigms of male muses. It may be useful for the purposes of this essay to refer to the opening poem in Elizabeth Barrett Browning's *Sonnets from the Portuguese*. By comparing Browning's first sonnet with Stone's poems quoted above, it seems plausible to misinterpret the male muse who appears as death. In Browning, the muse's disembodied voice, split from the female poet's musing, confirms in the concluding line that "his" identity, rather than death, is love. A "mystic Shape" appears out of the shadows, and the poet gradually envisions a masculine presence, who, in a brutal gesture, takes the speaker "by the hair" and queries: "'Guess now who holds thee?'—'Death,' I said. But, there, / The silver answer rang,—'Not Death, but Love'" (674). What could be a more conventional muse than love? Yet the comparison between Browning's sonnet and Stone's poems reveals a major difference:

Browning, whose sequence was addressed to a living male muse
(her future husband), remains within the female poet/male muse
paradigm; Stone's poems, however, which seem to posit the male
muse, in reality refer to a widow's transition from one phase of
mourning to another (anger, denial, acceptance, and transformation), which culminates in her celebration of widowhood. One
poem delineates more than any other the phase of mourning associated with anger: "Denouement." In a brief dramatic space, the
poem explodes with the poet's merciless accusation toward the
"other" who left her in this "hell" on earth with the "hundred eyes"
that "saw [her] on fire." Here, the allusion to suttee appears in
Stone's poetry for the first time:

> You intimidated me. I was thrown into hell without a trial.
> Guilty by default. It was clear the murdered one was dead.
> There were only two of us. But no one came to lead me
>   away.
> A hundred eyes looked in and saw me on fire.
> We loved him, they said. Then they forgot.
> After many years I knew who it was who had died.
> Murderer, I whispered, you tricked me.
>
> > *(S-HC 97)*

"Denouement" supplies the evidence, the verbal proof, of her rage,
and the title implies an unraveling of the widow's identity as well
as her burgeoning sense of guilt.

The dramatic revelation begins with the innocent speaker's indict-
ment of the guilty party. Recalling another tragic love story, that
of Orpheus and Eurydice, the opening voice in "Denouement" says,
"You intimidated me. I was thrown into hell without a trial. / Guilty
by default." Left to survive, abandoned and forgotten, she evokes
associations not only to suttee but also to the cultural realities of
social ostracism and loneliness a widow experiences: "A hundred
eyes looked in and saw me on fire." Mourners gape, offer their
condolences, and leave the widow—who neither screams nor cries
but whispers in a barely audible rage—to remember the one who
is "dead."

Aspects of this phase (guilt and "searching for a lost spouse," or "sensing the 'presence' of the deceased spouse" [DeGuilio 106]) can be found in other poems by Stone. For instance, guilt resurfaces in one more poem in *Who Is the Widow's Muse?* The widow queries:

> was I involved
> in my darling's demise?
> The result of this inner
> flagellation
> was a headache.
>
> (*WM* 47)

And the survivor numbs her guilt with a sedative. Or, as we move with a muse who will evolve as something beyond the bird / crow / anima of a classical muse, we are warned not to confuse the spouse for a muse. In a mocking "search for a lost spouse," the widow's muse will not share identities with the dead spouse:

> The muse is mad.
> It keeps digging him up
> to check his identity.
>
> (*WM* 45)

Readers are warned in the prologue poem of a "rune" in which an enigmatic secret will be revealed. Initially, "All Time Is Past Time" hints about a solitary bird / muse / spirit connected to an anonymous biblical widow in their mutual quest for a transformation miraculously connected to the absurdity of time. ("The stone turns into a bird. . . . / This is the bird singing alone. . . . / She is the stone and the bird" [*WM* prologue].) Embedded in a mythical river of patriarchal forgetfulness, the immortal "Stone" is buried no less than five times in the four stanzas,[2] and we are reminded of the biblical incident in which David slew Goliath with a "chosen stone."

Stone's oracular voice manipulates the verses into a transparent contemporary lyric in which she invokes Tamar, the first biblical widow, and, in one leap, also alludes to the opening words in the New Testament's Gospel of John, "In the beginning was the Word." I quote the entire poem:

Goliath is struck by the stone.
The stone turns into a bird.
The bird sings in her window.
Time is absurd. It flows backward.
It is married to the word.

This is the window of the giant's eyes.
This is the bird singing alone.
This is the river of forgetting.
This is the chosen stone.
This is Goliath's widow.

Struck by the stone he leaps
into the future. He lies
a monolith, a rune, light
from a distant nova. Not even a bone
remembers begetting him ever.

The song is a monotone.
She is the word and the window.
She is the stone and the bird.
She is the bed of the river.

(*WM* prologue)

This narrative incorporates all the elements of time, past, present, and future.

In the beginning, at least the beginning that preoccupies Ruth Stone, is the act of biblical revisioning; she dedicates a hymn to a nameless widow, then continues to honor all widows as the quest begins. "The song is a monotone." Repeated over the centuries, the melody remains constant: the widow always sings the same song, in a deceptively simple yet cryptic form, which, in Hélène Cixous's words, "retains the power of moving us" (339). As for the future, the poet relegates the "rune" to a masculine realm ("Struck by the stone he leaps / into the future"). Memory, the muse, and mourning become less enigmatic if we associate memory with the "giant's eyes" and the ravens of Odin.

Goliath is relegated to a "distant nova." "Not even a bone / remembers begetting him ever." Not even the primal bone, which the poet defines as the most wondrous, glistening part of existence, remembers "begetting" or engendering "him." She subtly erases the overwhelming "he"—but does he represent the masculine muse? Or, is Stone giving a clue to her readers: is "he" simply the metaphor for all of the monolithic men in the poet's past?[3] One more enigma remains in this epilogue to the quest: why the poet's choice of Goliath and why the creation of Goliath's widow? Had she existed, no other widow would have inherited a more leprous legacy. But in a gesture of biblical revisioning, the poet has taken a leap from the Book of Ruth, perhaps the most lyrical biblical story ever written about two widows, to the Book of Samuel.

"She is the word and the window." Illuminations, visions, windows of clarity. The "she" is a multiple "she": the poet envisions a legacy for all widows of the world, from the past to the present into the future.

> "Am I, then, the widow's muse?"
> cries the widow.
> "Is alone more alone
> than I was led to believe?"
>
> (*WM* 9)

Even though muses come in all personalities and guises, Stone's muse in this poetic sequence is interrogative and playful, philosophical and lyrical, problematic and provocative. Stone's muse is a reimagining of the muses in their multiplicity as she couples the inflammatory word of muse with the dangerous word of widow. Did she breach a male literary taboo by joining them together?

Rather than live with an "absent muse," Stone creates a lively muse who is devilishly cynical, who fluctuates from mad to maternal, who evaporates and sighs with exhaustion, who becomes objectified as, among other things, a car, a frog, a fetish.

Gradually, however, a "being" emerges and we discover a teacher-muse who guides the widow through her mourning to a moment of celebration. The dialogue between the two is actually the inspirational force that teaches the widow to clarify the meaning of the spouse's loss, to place mourning in perspective, and to return to "The blood and meat of the world" (*WM* 59). In the quest for a clearly defined muse, we encounter the muse as bird (in "All Time Is Past Time") or "crow" (1) or "anima": "Is my claim to the muse /

no more than my own breath?" (14). Perhaps the most comical
muse appears in poem 31 in which a clue surfaces that the muse is
a "courier" somewhere between Rensselaer and Albany, New York:[4]
"'The widow's muse is a city-pigeon,' / the rising widow murmured"
(35). One more poem indicates the muse as a go-between for something, but an intermediary for what specifically? The "rune" continues. Stone reflects, "Perhaps we are born widows. . . . Yes, the muse
is a key" (25). But a "key" to which mystery? To which realm of
knowledge? What is the muse concealing from the poet?

Does the muse have a determinable gender? A merging of identities—"they are me; / I am them" (32)—confuses us. The muse's
identity is undefined and fluctuates from an "it" to a "we":

> The muse let a single tear
> slip from its closed eyes.
> "We are not amused,"
> it muttered.
>
> (*WM* 32)

Slowly, the muse emerges as a "being" with emotions of envy or
shyness: "Could the widow's muse be envious?" (37). Stone defines
the gender of "it" in a poem about a poetry festival where five
hundred women are gathered to listen: "The widow's muse was at
the Festival, too. / She was the one with iron grey hair" (51).

The muse, in perpetual metamorphosis, ultimately appears as the
mother of muses in the final poem. She compassionately holds the
pleading widow ("'Just one more about shoes'" [59]) in her arms;
they repeat the reality of the spouse's death; and the reader is left
with the widow and her doppelgänger-muse, with the debris of
death and with the enduring love of one spouse for another. After
thirty years of mourning her loss, Ruth Stone's "love transcends
[her] despair" (*TOP* 98), and finally, transformation is near. I quote
the last poem in its entirety:

> The widow is told by a great seer
> that fifty-two is a magic number.
> She consults the muse.
> "We must get into a higher gear,"
> the muse whispers. "We must shift

out of this phase."
"Just one more about shoes,"
the widow begs.
The muse shakes her head.
"No. We must get back to the real thing.
The blood and meat of the world."
The muse took the widow in her arms.
"Now say it with me," the muse said.
"Once and for all . . . he is forever dead."

(*WM* 59)

Only questions edge the mind toward eternity. By acknowledging the quest for the muse, the poet posed no fewer than thirteen questions in search of "it," "he," or "she" in *Who Is the Widow's Muse?* The quest became a universal widow's journey as she liberated herself from her mourning to shift out of that phase into her metamorphosis: "So I am without number."

Notes

A skeletal version of this essay was presented at the SUNY Dead/Lines Conference (Buffalo, New York, 1993). I wish to thank Robert Daly and Gregory Norwin for their responses. And I'm particularly grateful to Leslie and Sally Fiedler, Genevieve James, and Kathleen Betsko Yale for their generous commentaries on subsequent drafts.

1. Sword and thorn are interchangeable symbols: "A stick fire / and a thorn for her body" (*WM* 1). No fewer than six of the eight paintings created by Phoebe Stone, which accompany her mother's poetry, contain a bright, orange flame, and in the crow/widow-in-flight image, a rose thorn penetrates the woman's body.

2. The poet symbolically inscribes her name five times in this poem, perhaps in memory of the five family members: Walter, Ruth, Marcia, Phoebe, and Abigail.

3. In poem 44, the muse disappears on vacation and corresponds with the widow: "Am playing tennis everyday with / Don Hall, Don Justice, Don Juan." The poem is also intriguing because of its phallic symbolism and the poet's pun on "a logical illogic" (*WM* 50).

4. The autobiographical element is inscribed here. "It was this time of year he died" (*WM* 35). Walter B. Stone died on 11 March 1959.

Works Cited

Browning, Elizabeth Barrett. *Sonnets from the Portuguese. The Norton Anthology of Poetry*. Ed. Alexander W. Allison et al. 3rd ed. New York: Norton, 1983. 674.

Cixous, Hélène. "The Laugh of the Medusa." *Feminisms, an Anthology of Literary Theory and Criticism*. Ed. Robyn R. Warhol and Diane Price Herndl. Rutgers: State University, 1991. 334–49.

Cooper, J. C. *An Illustrated Encyclopedia of Traditional Symbols*. New York: Thames, 1990.

DeGuilio, Robert. *Beyond Widowhood*. New York: Free, 1989.

DeShazer, Mary K. *Inspiring Women: Reimagining the Muse*. New York: Pergamon, 1986.

Friedman, Norman. "Ruth Stone." *Contemporary Poets*. 5th ed. Chicago and London: St. James, 1991. 965–66.

Hughes, Ted. *Crow*. New York: Harper, 1971.

The Jerusalem Bible. New York: Doubleday, 1968.

Schenck, Celeste. "All of a Piece: Women's Poetry and Autobiography." *Life/Lines, Theorizing Women's Autobiography*. Ed. Bella Brodzki and Celeste Schenck. Ithaca and London: Cornell UP, 1988. 292.

Scigaj, Leonard M. *The Poetry of Ted Hughes: Form and Imagination*. Iowa: U of Iowa P, 1986.

Virgil. *The Aeneid of Virgil*. Trans. C. Day Lewis. New York: Doubleday, 1953.

18 *Definitions of Love*
Ruth Stone's Feminist Caritas
Sandra M. Gilbert

The wind was shaking me all night long;
Shaking me in my sleep
Like a definition of love. . . .
> —Ruth Stone, "Green Apples"

. . . the word "love" is itself in need of re-vision.
> —Adrienne Rich, "When We Dead Awaken: Writing as Re-Vision"

Beginning perhaps most strikingly with the writings of Sylvia Plath, Adrienne Rich, Diane Wakoski, and Audre Lorde, much of the verse produced by the so-called second wave of feminism has been shaped by what Rich once defined as a "phenomenology of anger," with many of the strongest poems in this period functioning as, in Lorde's phrase, "cables to rage." Speaking of the "embattled" energy of Plath and Diane Wakoski, Rich observed in her classic "When We Dead Awaken" (1971) that "until recently this female anger and this furious awareness of the Man's power over her were not available materials to the female poet, who tended to write of Love as the source of her suffering, and to view that victimization by Love as an almost inevitable fate" (36). But "today," she added later in the piece, "much poetry by women . . . is charged with anger," noting that "we need to go through that anger, and we will betray our own reality if we try" for the sort of "objectivity" or "detachment" that Virginia Woolf recommended in *A Room of One's Own* (48, 49). As Rich herself was aware, these statements were both descriptions of what was happening in her own verse and prescriptions for what needed to happen to a number of artists if the reborn feminist movement was to have a significant aesthetic impact. Disturbing as it was to a range of readers, then, Plath's "Daddy, I have had to kill you . . . daddy, I'm finally through" (222, 224) has had to be reiterated by an army of dancing and stamping women, all seeking to exorcise the paternal demon at the heart of so many of our cultural institutions.

Yet in the same essay, Rich also declared, in a passage from which I have drawn one of my epigraphs, that "the word 'love' is itself in need of re-vision," of "seeing with fresh eyes" (35, 47). And that remark, though it is less frequently cited than the others I've quoted, aseems to me to be directly relevant to the extraordinary achievement of Ruth Stone. How can the word "love" be revised in an often unlovable world, a world that evokes "female anger" and "furious awareness of Man's power"? What might *feminist* love mean for a poet living and writing in such a world? I would argue that for Ruth Stone, love is not primarily a "source of . . . suffering" nor is "victimization by Love . . . an almost inevitable fate." Instead, "love" means quite simply *caritas*—charity—in the old sense, a charity that never flinches at the hardest facts but that can forgive sources of suffering even while naming and renaming them precisely because the poet is not victimized by love, she is in control of it.

Let me say at once that, as a longtime friend and admirer of Ruth's, I think she has had just about as many reasons to be "angry" as anyone I know, and I am certain that those who are familiar with her work will agree with me. Yet her other admirers will also agree that, if and when she reads this statement, she would say— she *will* say—*But I have as many reasons to rejoice as anyone you know, Sandra*. One key to her art is the generosity with which Ruth converts specifics that might merely elicit rage into the details of an imaginative empathy akin to Keatsian "negative capability." In fact, as Rich suggested a woman poet should, Ruth has unprogrammatically lived "through" her anger and come out on the other side in the spirit of *caritas*. Often Dickinsonian in its terseness and inventiveness, her poetry is also Whitmanesque in the elasticity of its sympathies, in its willingness to accept the catalog of differences—the second-hand coats, the trailer parks and the tract houses, the lovers, the children and grandchildren—that this artist encounters on open roads and back roads as she buses around our country.

From aging Mrs. Dubosky to ferocious Aunt Maud, from the hospital-going Masons to Mr. Tempesta the "nervous" landlord, the figures Ruth confronts in her poems are objects of love and compassion, not of anger or contempt. As the

> ten o'clock train to New York . . .
> . . . passes a station;
> fresh people standing on the platform,
> their faces expecting something

she states her creed: "I feel their entire histories ravish me" (*S-HC* 18). And the particularity of such sensitivity surely underlies Ruth's resistance to any dogmatism, even to a dogmatically angry feminism. As she writes in her hilarious "Some Things You'll Need to Know Before You Join the Union,"

> The antiwar and human rights poems
> are processed in the white room.
> Everyone in there wears sterile gauze.
> These poems go for a lot.
> No one wants to mess up.
> There's expensive equipment involved,
> The workers have to be heavy,
> very heavy.
> These poems are packaged in cement.
> You frequently hear them drop with a dull thud.
>
> (*S-HC* 49)

No matter how righteous it may be, Ruth implies, one kind of coercion is no substitute for another, and righteousness itself must be revised if it is to prevail.

Some of Ruth's best-known poems are, of course, proudly and explicitly feminist works in which she celebrates the matrilineage that gave her the strength to love. Even while mourning the lost names of mothers and grandmothers, for instance, "Names" rejoices in the heritage transmitted by those ancestresses: "In me are all the names I can remember—pennyroyal, boneset, / bedstraw, toad-flax—from whom I did descend in perpetuity" (*S-HC* 23). Similarly,

"Pokeberries" affirms "the Virginia mountains . . . my grandma's pansy bed . . . my Aunt Maud's dandelion wine" along with a fiercely revisionary Eve: "my mama, who didn't just bite an apple / with her big white teeth. She split it in two" (*S-HC* 11). At the same time, though, "How Aunt Maud Took to Being a Woman" laughs both at and with Aunt Maud, who "was a vengeful house-keeper," and shows considerable sympathy to Uncle Cal, who "spent a lot of time on the back porch / waiting to be let in" (*S-HC* 32). For, as Ruth Stone remembers them, her male relatives and ancestors are rarely demons who require exorcism but instead are fellow inhabitants of that cosmos in which we must all "go down the long stairway / Into the dark coal sack of the sky" (*S-HC* 113).

In this regard, a virtually paradigmatic Stone poem is *"Liebeslied,"* a delicate love song written when Ruth was living in a rented room in the Sacramento valley. Attending to the details of the quotidian—"the landlord's child" who "cries at night, / in the next room," "a female cat / who lives wild / among these tract houses," and out on the "cement patio" the child's "toy truck / stopped in its forward surge / just where it is / loaded with mildewed walnuts"—the poet notes the poignancy of the domestic and remembers, without blame or rage, her father, "whistling late at night":

> He is walking along Irvington Avenue
> from the streetcar line.
> Alone, downstairs
> he winds up the phonograph—
> at the wavering edge
> Fritz Kreisler's *Liebeslied.*
> I listen in the dark
> to the bowed strings of sadness and pain
> to what the human voice
> beyond itself
> is telling me.
>
> (*S-HC* 13–14)

"What the human voice . . . / is telling me": to hear that still sad music, a woman must perhaps live through and beyond anger—anger at the father, anger at the landlord, anger at the tract houses—and arrive at an outpost of culture where both clarity and charity are possible. And indeed, if the landlords who show up here and there in Stone's poems are oppressive, they are also treated with mercy, as in the wonderful stretch villanelle "Surviving in Earlysville with a Broken Window," whose Mr. Garvey refuses to make repairs because, in a comically reiterated refrain, he "tells me old window glass is frail." Villain that he is (he "lives in Charlottesville, receives my rent by mail"), Mr. Garvey is also just another term in an absurd economic chain ("A man dealing in cattle has use of his fields, steers graze / his worn out acres. / . . . The cattle dealer is starving the cattle while Mr. Garvey / receives my rent by mail") so that his stubborn predations elicit from the poet a monitory statement of *caritas*:

> I'm vegetarian, talk to the steers. I say we must love
>   each other and the great blue whale
> and the gone silly dodo who helpfully scored in its
>   gizzard the thick endocarps of the, for all purposes now,
>   extinct calvaria tree; coevolution of seed and seed breaker.
>
>   (*S-HC* 43)

Mr. Garvey, Ruth Stone implies, needs not theatrical exorcism but knowledge of his place in an ecology that may at some point abandon him as surely as it has the "gone silly dodo."

When I asked Ruth once about the relationship between fury and forgiveness in her work, she said that hers were poems of "desperate love," and that self-defining statement is nowhere more true than in the pieces she has written about her dead husband. As countless poems in *Topography*, *Cheap*, and *Second-Hand Coat* attest, a man who hangs himself, leaving behind a wife and three children, must be, to say the least, a source of suffering—suffering *from* what he has done as well as suffering *for* him. Yet because in her art Ruth has moved with stern control through the stages of grief and rage, because, as one reviewer recently put it, her mourning has become electric, her lost husband has consistently functioned as what she has called "the widow's muse." An absent presence, the man who must be forgiven for his pain *and* her pain has become a silent interlocutor in a continuing dialogue that illuminates both the gravity and the levity of fate. "It is your skeleton I crave," Ruth tells him severely in one poem:

> the way the bones of your feet,
> fitted like the wing sockets of angels,
> came toward me in time over the long
> plateaus of ice; their delicate mouselike tread
> printed in tracks of snow over my mind.
>
> (*S-HC* 42)

But in another, as, impersonating "my Aunt Virginia, / proud but weak in the head," she persuades the nervous landlord Mr. Tempesta to let her keep her two cats, she speaks to the dead man with comic triumph:

> I want to dig you up and say, look,
> it's like the time, remember,
> when I ran into our living room naked
> to get rid of that fire inspector.
>
> See what you miss by being dead?
>
> (*S-HC* 15)

If there is anger here—and I don't doubt that there is—it is anger that strains toward forgiveness, anger that seeks not to dance and stamp on love but to find some way of resurrecting it, if only through the mercy of the imagination.

What fuels Ruth Stone's impulse toward mercy? I would say that one source of her "desperate love" is maternity. Ruth Stone—like Sylvia Plath, Anne Sexton, and Denise Levertov, among many others—is one of a group of poet-mothers for whom creativity and maternity do not seem to be contradictory terms. On the one hand, unlike a number of her nineteenth-century precursors, Ruth hasn't apparently felt constrained by an ideology of domesticity that would require her to sentimentalize the experience of motherhood. On the other hand, unlike a number of her modernist predecessors, she hasn't found it necessary to repudiate the role of mother. Instead, she writes to and about her children—facts of her life and art—as directly and lucidly as she would about any other subject. They are *there*, not to be glamorized but not to be ignored. And the continuing empathy along with the alternating passions of delight and despair that they evoke, as all children do, widen from a mother-bond into a bond with a larger population.

Addressing her "Dear children" in "Advice," for example, this poet is also, of course, addressing *us*:

> Dear children, you must try to say
> Something when you are in need.
> Don't confuse hunger with greed;
> And don't wait until you are dead.
>
> (*S-HC* 112)

And in "End of Summer . . . 1969," a letter to "Dear Phoebe, wherever you are," "Dear Marcia," and "Dear Abigail" broadens into one of the loving letters to the world that I quoted from earlier:

> Dear Mother, and sisters and brothers, dear nieces,
> All at once proclaim in a loud voice
> Summer is over. In the traces
> Of broken stars it is too late for truces and wars.
> You must go down the long stairway
> Into the dark coal sack of the sky.
>
> (*S-HC* 113)

To be sure, one of Ruth Stone's most successful poems is the sardonic "Song of Absinthe Granny," whose speaker remembers her domestic past with comic weariness:

> Among some hills there dwelt in parody
> A young woman; me.
> I was that gone with child
> That before I knew it I had three
> And they hung whining and twisting. . . .
> Three pips that plagued the life out of me.
>
> (*S-HC* 86)

Isn't Absinthe Granny hilariously narcissistic?

> My birds have flocked,
> And I'm old and wary.
> I'm old and worn and a cunning sipper,
> And I'll outlive every little nipper.
> And with what's left I'm chary,
> And with what's left I'm chary.
>
> (*S-HC* 88)

And doesn't Ruth Stone's celebration of such witty solipsism in some sense controvert my claim that her poems are definitions of love?

I would say no, and in support of my reply I would point to the etymological connection between "chariness" and "charity": both words derive from a root that means (albeit in various ways) "dear." To be chary is to *hold* things "dear"; to be charitable is to *find* things "dear." And for Ruth it is what Gerard Manley Hopkins called "The dearest freshness deep down things" ("God's Grandeur") that must be found, held, praised. As the widening sphere possessed by her definitions of love reaches to encircle even a "dark coal sack" of pain and grief, she blesses victims and villains alike. In the beautiful "The Latest Hotel Guest Walks over Particles That Revolve in Seven Other Dimensions Controlling Latticed Space," the object of Ruth Stone's desperate love is an innocent "android" sculpted out of

> . . . the escaped molecules,
> radiation photons and particulate particles
> of the hair and skin of all [the] former guests
>
> . . . .
> . . . an antihero composed of all the lost neutrinos

who might be "programmed to weep and beat its head / and shout, 'Which war? . . . How much?'" (*S-HC* 40).

In the even more beautiful "Translations," that object of affection is the more culpable Alexander Mehielovitch Touritzen, a vulgar and bizarre onetime lover whose part in the Second World War the poet cannot decipher:

> Where were you when they fed the multitudes to the ovens?
> Old fetid fisheyes, did they roll you in at the cannery?
> Did you build their bridges or blow them up?
> Are you burned to powder? Were you mortarized?
> Did you die in a ditch, Mehielovitch? Are you exorcized?
> (*S-HC* 54–55)

Yet whether he was guilty or not, Ruth Stone translates Mehielovitch, with Rilke-esque generosity, into a soul deserving that maternal and feminist *caritas*, which is one of the sources not of her suffering but of her genius.

> Poor innocent lecher, you believed in sin.
> I see you rising with the angels, thin forgotten dirty-fingered
>   son
> of a silk stocking factory owner in Constantinople,
> may you be exonerated. May you be forgiven.
> May you be a wax taper in paradise,
> Alexander Mehielovitch Touritzen.
>
>   (*S-HC* 55)

For Ruth Stone, the vegetables in "the cutting room" (*C* 33), the man who wants to be "a stallion," "the wild mares" who "come up out of the night fields" (*C* 54), and the bulls and birds who cry "out of their separateness. / This is the way it is. This is the way it is" (*C* 46)—all in their distinctive fashions propose the dearest freshness of disparate energies, particulate particles. She tells us that every tree found a way to the light as did every other creature, from her dead father and her dead husband to the living children, all of us, who must not "confuse hunger with greed" (*TOP* 89).

And such dearness inevitably inspires not anger but the joy of *caritas*. When I asked Ruth why her blessing of Mehielovitch was entitled "Translations," she explained that in *this* "*Liebeslied*" she was translating "another language, of the male world. . . . translating . . . the knowledge I have picked up here and there about war and human behavior." Translating, I would say, as a mother might, a mother who does not define herself as oppressed and marginalized but instead as central, powerful, a link in the ongoing, perpetually changing chain of generations, a mother—and daughter and lover— who has learned how to revise the word "love." Let me quote in full the poem "Green Apples," from which I drew part of my title:

> In August we carried the old horsehair mattress
> To the back porch
> And slept with our children in a row.
> The wind came up the mountain into the orchard
> Telling me something;
> Saying something urgent.
> I was happy.

The green apples fell on the sloping roof
And rattled down.
The wind was shaking me all night long;
Shaking me in my sleep
Like a definition of love,
Saying, this is the moment,
Here, now.

(TOP 37)

Works Cited

Plath, Sylvia. *The Collected Poems*. New York: Harper, 1981.
Rich, Adrienne. *On Lies, Secrets, and Silence: Selected Prose 1966–1978*. New York: Norton, 1979.

Contributors
Index

Contributors

Wendy Barker is a professor of English at the University of Texas at San Antonio. She has published two collections of poems, *Winter Chickens* (1990) and *Let the Ice Speak* (1991). A chapbook, *Poems from Paradise*, is forthcoming. Also author of *Lunacy of Light: Emily Dickinson and the Experience of Metaphor* (1987), she has completed a third book of poems, *Way of Whiteness*, and is working on a fourth book of poems, *Generation*.

Aliki Barnstone is an assistant professor of English at Bucknell University. Her volumes of poems include *Windows in Providence* (1981), and *Cavafy in the Early Morning* and *Bright Snow* (both forthcoming). She has coedited *A Book of Women Poets from Antiquity to Now* (1980, 1992) and *The Calvinist Roots of the Modern Era* (forthcoming).

Willis Barnstone is Distinguished Professor of Comparative Literature at Indiana University. Among his over two dozen books are *Sappho and the Greek Lyric Poets* (1962), *The Other Bible* (1984), *The Poetics of Translation* (1993), *The Secret Reader: 501 Sonnets* (1995), and *Sunday Morning in Fascist Spain* (1995). A translator of ancient and modern poets including Sappho, Wang Wei, and Borges, he has also published eight collections of his own poetry and has twice been nominated for the Pulitzer Prize in Poetry.

Elyse Blankley is an associate professor of English and women's studies at California State University, Long Beach. She has published essays in *Women Writers in the City* (1984) and *Critical Essays on Gertrude Stein* (1986) and is currently working on a study of female transgression in turn-of-the-century American and British novels.

Robert Bradley's poetry and criticism have appeared in *Plough-shares*, *Gettysburg Review*, *Southern Poetry Review*, *Painted Bride Quarterly*, *Antioch Review*, and *Seneca Review*, as well as in other journals. He is also the editor of Haw River Books, publishers of poetry by Ruth Stone, William Stafford, and other poets.

Kevin Clark is an associate professor of English at California Polytechnic State University. He has published essays in *The Iowa Review*, *Papers on Language & Literature*, and *American Poetry*, and he has writen two chapbooks of poetry, *Granting the Wolf* (1984) and *Widow under a New Moon* (1990).

Leslie Fiedler holds the Samuel P. Clemens Chair at the State University of New York at Buffalo where he is a Distinguished Professor of English. He has authored numerous influential books on American literature, including *An End to Innocence: Essays on Culture and Politics* (1955), *Love and Death in the American Novel* (1960), *Freaks* (1978), and *What Was Literature?: Class Culture and Mass Society* (1982).

Jan Freeman is the author of two collections of poetry, *Autumn Sequence* (1993) and *Hyena* (1993). She is completing a new collection of poems, *Tenderness*.

Norman Friedman is a professor emeritus of English at Queens College, City University of New York, and a private practitioner and teacher of Gestalt psychotherapy. He has published books on E. E. Cummings (1960, 1964) and has another volume forthcoming. His *Form and Meaning in Fiction* appeared in 1975. He has also published two collections of poems, *The Magic Badge* (1984) and *The Intrusions of Love* (1992).

Roger Gilbert is an associate professor of English at Cornell University. He is the author of a number of essays on contemporary poetry and other topics, as well as a book, *Walks in the World: Representation and Experience in Modern American Poetry* (1991). He is at work on a study of the contemporary long poem.

Sandra M. Gilbert is a professor of English at the University of California, Davis, and the author of five collections of poetry, most recently *Ghost Volcano* (1995), and a memoir, *Wrongful Death: A Medical Tragedy* (1995), as well as a number of critical works. With Susan Gubar, she has coauthored *The Madwoman in the Attic: The Woman Writer and the Nineteenth-Century Literary Imagination* (1979) and *No Man's Land: The Place of the Woman Writer in the Twentieth Century*, Vols. 1, 2, and 3 (1987, 1988, 1994), and coedited several other volumes, including *The Norton Anthology of Literature by Women: The Tradition in English* (1985).

Kandace Brill Lombart is currently completing her doctoral dissertation on Ruth Stone under the guidance of Leslie Fiedler at the State University of New York at Buffalo. She is coediting a book on women playwrights.

Janet Lowery is an assistant professor of English at the University of St. Thomas. A chapbook of her poetry, *Thin Dimes*, was published in 1992.

Diana O'Hehir is a professor emeritus of English at Mills College. Her first collection of poetry, *Summoned* (1976), won the Devins Award for Poetry. Subsequent books include *The Power to Change Geography* (1979) and several novels, including *I Wish This War Were Over* (1984), *Home Free* (1988), and *The Bride Who Ran Away* (1989). A forthcoming collection of poems is titled *Spells for Not Dying Again*.

Sharon Olds directs the Creative Writing Program at New York University and is the founding chair of the Writing Program at Goldwater Hospital for the Severely Disabled. Her collections of poetry include *Satan Says* (1980), for which she received the San Francisco Poetry Center Award, *The Dead and the Living* (1984), which won the Lamont Poetry Prize and the National Book Critics Circle Award, *The Gold Cell* (1987), and *The Father* (1992). Her latest collection, *The Wellspring*, is forthcoming in 1996.

Martha Nell Smith is an associate professor of English at the University of Maryland, College Park. She is the author of *Rowing in Eden: Rereading Emily Dickinson* (1992) and, with Suzanne Juhasz and Cristanne Miller, *Comic Power in Emily Dickinson* (1993). With Ellen Louise Hart, she is completing *The Book of Susan and Emily Dickinson* and, with Jonnie Guerra, *Titanic Operas: American Women's Poetry and the Influence of Dickinson*.

Diane Wakoski is the Writer in Residence at Michigan State University, where she is also a University Distinguished Professor. She has published twenty collections of poetry, including *The George Washington Poems* (1967), *The Motorcycle Betrayal Poems* (1971), *Why My Mother Likes Liberace* (1985), and a volume of selected poems, *Emerald Ice*, which won the William Carlos Williams Prize in 1990. Her newest collection, *The Emerald City of Las Vegas*, is forthcoming.

Index

DATE DUE